Aladdin Systems is committed to providing the best customer support in the business.

We're willing to back up those words with a range of services that go beyond most other manufacturers.
Our registered users can take advantage of free technical support, reasonable upgrades, training, advance product announcements and bulletins. In addition, Aladdin Systems sponsors Academic, User Group and Corporate Programs.

30-Day Money-Back Guarantee.
We are confident that you will like every Aladdin Systems product. However, if you are dissatisfied with this product, you may return it for a full refund. Write or call us for more information.

If you have any problems using this product, we recommend the following:
Review the manual – it answers most questions and problems. If you still have a question, you may contact us by any of the methods below. If you choose to call, please have your manual and original program disk(s) on hand. Also, being seated at your computer with the program running will help us serve you better.

Mailing Address	**Technical Support Hotline**
Aladdin Systems, Inc.	(408) 761-6200
Customer Support Group	(408) 761-6206 fax
165 Westridge Drive	Monday - Friday
Watsonville, CA 95076	9 am - 5 pm PST

On-line
AppleLink, America Online: ALADDIN
GEnie: ALADDINSYS
CompuServe: 75300,1666
Internet: aladdin@well.sf.ca.us

If you have any comments or suggestions, please feel free to contact us by any of the above methods. We welcome your input.

Registration Number: B62976

D1122167

Registration Card:
By registering, you are entitled to free technical support and upgrade notices. Please take a few moments to complete and mail this postage-paid card. (Remove this portion before mailing.)

Please write legibly and complete entire card.

Name _____

Company (if applicable) _____

Address _____

City _____ State _____ Zip/Postal Code _____ Country _____

Daytime telephone _____ Fax _____

Where can we reach you online? _____

Please send me informaton on: ☐ Site licenses ☐ Volume purchases

Place purchased _____ Date purchased ___ / ___ / ___

Which other Aladdin products do you own? _____

Where did you hear about StuffIt Deluxe 3.0?
☐ Friend ☐ Dealer ☐ Ad in _____
☐ User group ☐ Trade show ☐ Other _____

Macintosh owned
Printer _____
Modem speed _____
RAM memory _____
Hard disk? ☐ Yes ☐ No   Networked? ☐ Yes ☐ No
Modem? ☐ Yes ☐ No   Use E-Mail? ☐ Yes ☐ No

Occupation _____

People in company: ☐ 1-9 ☐ 10-49 ☐ 50-99 ☐ 100+

StuffIt Deluxe 3.0 7/92

B62976

BUSINESS REPLY MAIL

FIRST CLASS MAIL PERMIT NO. 14 WATSONVILLE CA

POSTAGE WILL BE PAID BY ADDRESSEE

ALADDIN SYSTEMS INC
165 WESTRIDGE DR
WATSONVILLE CA 95076-9910

Your Comments:

Please take a moment to let us know what you think about StuffIt Deluxe 3.0. By completing this questionnaire and returning it to us, you will be providing us with valuable information we can use to produce even better products in the future. We value your comments just as we value your business.

StuffIt Deluxe 3.0: If you have any comments or suggestions, please contact us by sending us this postage-paid card. We welcome your input.

What do you like about StuffIt Deluxe 3.0?

What don't you like about StuffIt Deluxe 3.0?

What are the most important features of this software?

What are the least important features of this software?

What would you like to see in the future?

StuffIt Deluxe 3.0 7/92

BUSINESS REPLY MAIL
FIRST CLASS MAIL PERMIT NO. 14 WATSONVILLE CA

POSTAGE WILL BE PAID BY ADDRESSEE

ALADDIN SYSTEMS INC
165 WESTRIDGE DR
WATSONVILLE CA 95076-9910

StuffIt Deluxe
A User's Guide

August 1992

Aladdin Systems, Inc.
165 Westridge Drive
Watsonville, California 95076

Manual by Michael Miley and David Schargel.

Software written by: Raymond Lau, Dawson Dean, Leonard Rosenthol, Marco A. Gonzalez, and Darryl Lovato.

Special thanks to: Cindy Briggs, Marshall Clow, Greg Friedman, Robert Gibson, Alexandra Gonzalez, Thomas Haller, David Heffron, Jane Hendriksen, Nancy Homyak, Mike Isbell and Sun Litho, Jonathan Kahn, Ron Kashden, Mark Kawakami, Brad Kollmyer, Serge Limondin, Benná Lovato, C. Joseph Marini, Mika Color, Jane Natoli, Kristina Solomon, Stephan Somogyi, Rodney Tao, Paul B. Taubman II, Terry Teague, Brad Tempelton, Robert Ulrich, Janet Viets, our beta testers, and you, for purchasing this product.

Colophon

The type used is Courier, ITC Century Condensed and Zapf Dingbats. Text and graphics were generated using Microsoft Word and Canvas. Layout was done with FrameMaker and pages were proofed using an Apple LaserWriter NTX. Final pages were generated on a Linotronic 200P. Special credit goes to QT/Snipper.

Table of Contents

Chapter 1: Introduction...7
    Welcome 7
    How to use this Manual...7
    Manual Conventions..8
    A Primer 9
    Introduction..9
    Compression: Saving Space on Disk 9
    Archiving: The Basics of Combining Files and Folders 10
    Security: Protecting Files from Others.....................10
    SpaceSaver Defined 10
    Magic Menu Defined 11
    StuffIt Deluxe Defined 11
    The Extensions Defined..12
    Automating StuffIt...13
    UnStuffIt Defined 13
    A Note About System 6 and System 7 13
    Balloon Help...14

Chapter 2: Installation...15
    Requirements..15
    Easy Installation..15
    Custom Installation..19
    Where is StuffIt Deluxe Installed?.............................21
    Where to Go From Here 22

Chapter 3: Using StuffIt SpaceSaver..........................23
    Section One: Manual Compression.............................23
    Ways to Save Space...23
    Example: Compressing Folders...................................23
    Example: Compressing Individual Files......................25

Example: Sending a Folder to a Friend.................................26
Example: Expanding Multiple Items.....................................27
Section Two: Automatic Compression..................................28
Idle Time Compression..28
Example: Automatically Compressing Your Hard Disk.......29
Section Three: Mastering SpaceSaver & Magic Menu.........32
Preferences..32
The SpaceSaver Control Panel...32
Control Panel General Preferences......................................33
Control Panel Compression Preferences.............................35
Idle Time Compression Preferences....................................40
Magic Menu Compression Preferences...............................40
Where to Go From Here...43

Chapter 4: Using StuffIt Deluxe 45
Section One: The Basics of StuffIt.......................................45
Example: Stuffing a File...45
Example: Selectively UnStuffing from an Archive..............49
Where To Go From Here..53
Section Two: Beyond the Basics..53
Example: Creating Your Monthly and Yearly Archives......54
Example: Backing Up Your Yearly Archive.........................61
Example: Securing Files for Sending....................................64
Example: Self-Extracting Archives.....................................67
Section Three: Mastering StuffIt Deluxe.............................68
Close-up: The Open and Save As Dialogs............................68
Close-up: The Archive Palette and Window........................70
Close-up: Getting/Keeping Information on Archives...........77
Close-up: The Add Match Dialog..81
Close-up: Setting Your Preferences.....................................84
Where To Go From Here..95

Chapter 5: The Viewers Extensions.............................97
Introduction..97
Example: Sending a Print Job to a Service Bureau.............97
Text Viewer: Menus Defined..100
PICT Viewer: Menus Defined...104
Where To Go From Here...105

Chapter 6: Network/Communications.....................107
Introduction..107

Section One: Using StuffIt to Translate Files 107
Example: The Service Bureau 107
Section Two: Magic Menu and Electronic Mail 124
Example: Mailing Archives on a LAN 124
Section Three: StuffIt and Telecommunications 129
Microphone II Scripts 129
White Knight 131
Where To Go From Here 134

Chapter 7: The Tools/Utilities 135

Introduction 135
Hooking up with the Finder and Drop Boxes 135
Example: Stuffing with Drop•Stuff............................135
Example: UnStuffing with Drop•UnStuff..........................136
Hooking up with the Finder and Magic Menu 137
Example: Point & Click Stuffing from the Finder 137
Expand from Magic Menu..138
Compress from Magic Menu......................................139
Stuff from Magic Menu...140
Make Self-Extracting..140
Magic Menu Compression Preferences............................141
About Magic Menu… 144
StuffIt Converter...145
Example: Converting Older Archives 145
StuffIt XTND..147
Example: Using On Location with StuffIt Archives............147
Where To Go From Here 150

Chapter 8: Automating StuffIt....................................151

Section One:Scripting Within StuffIt..........................151
Example: Scripting Your Monthly Archive.......................151
Recording a Script..152
Editing a Script..155
Executing a Script 157
Adding a Script to the Menu 158
Removing a Script from the Menu...............................160
Example: Scripting Your Yearly Archive 160
Where To Go From Here 164
Section Two: Automating StuffIt From Outside 164
Apple events..165
QuicKeys 2..165

Example: Using Macros to Automate Archiving 165
HyperCard XCMDs...168
MPW Tools...169

Chapter 9: UnStuffIt...171

Introduction to UnStuffIt...171
Installation...171
Example: Opening SpaceSaver Files within UnStuffIt 171
Example: UnStuffing from StuffIt Archives 172
Example: Joining Segmented files....................................172
More about UnStuffIt 173

Chapter 10: Scripting Reference 175

Introduction 175
Scripting Rules 175
Helper Words 176
Wildcards..177
Variables...177
The Scripting Commands 178

Appendix: Common Questions (and Answers!)....187

General Questions 187
StuffIt SpaceSaver Questions.....................................189
StuffIt Deluxe Questions..190

Index 195

Chapter 1: Introduction

Welcome

Welcome to StuffIt Deluxe™, the complete compression solution for the Macintosh. Long-time users of StuffIt who are already accustomed to StuffIt's power will welcome this new, enhanced version of the product, and newcomers will be especially pleased. We've made some of StuffIt's newest features very easy to use. If it's your first time using StuffIt, you'll be up and running before you know it. You'll soon be wondering how you got along without it.

The StuffIt Deluxe package consists of the StuffIt SpaceSaver™ control panel, the Magic Menu™ control panel, the StuffIt Deluxe application, and the various extensions to the StuffIt application. This chapter will explain each of these items and provide you with an overview of what you should expect the software to do.

SpaceSaver helps you save disk space by compressing files and folders and allows you to use those files while they are compressed. With SpaceSaver, compression can occur selectively at your command or automatically while your computer is not being used.

How to use this Manual

This manual is organized by tasks and by the steps you'll go through to accomplish those tasks. The tasks are grouped according to the kind of compressing and archiving you may be doing. You can locate the task you have in mind by looking at the Table of Contents and at the Index, where subjects are listed under several terms you might associate with your task.

This chapter, **Chapter 1, Introduction**, is a primer on compression, archiving, and security. We also outline the main components of the StuffIt Deluxe package and why they're used.

Chapter 2, Installation, shows you how to install StuffIt Deluxe in the standard way or to customize the installation to your liking.

Chapter 3, Using SpaceSaver, shows you how to use the SpaceSaver control panel for transparent compression. Users who have already bought

SpaceSaver as a separate package and who have upgraded to StuffIt Deluxe will already recognize this chapter—it's identical to the manual they already have—so they can skip it. Everyone else should read it to learn about compressing from the Finder.

Chapter 4, Using StuffIt Deluxe, shows you how to use StuffIt Deluxe to archive your files and folders. Here we get down to business and show you the different ways you can use the program. From saving space, to archiving, to backup, to security, users will find what they need here to get the most out of StuffIt Deluxe.

Chapter 5, The Viewer Extensions, shows you how to use the Viewer Extensions for viewing text and PICT documents.

Chapter 6, Network and Communication Extensions, shows you how to translate files from different archival programs and other computer platforms, as well as how to use StuffIt with both electronic mail and telecommunication software.

Chapter 7, The Tools and Utility Extensions, shows you how to use the various tools and utilities that come with StuffIt Deluxe.

Chapter 8, Automating StuffIt, shows you how to automate StuffIt using StuffIt's scripting language or one of the useful Extensions to other software that we provide. You can use the Scripting language to build automated routines for archiving and backup. Scripts are very easy to build with a Record Script that will watch every action you do and record it into a script.

Chapter 9, UnStuffIt, shows you how to use the UnStuffit application to open SpaceSaver files, UnStuff StuffIt archives, and join segmented files.

Chapter 10, Scripting Reference, gives you a complete reference of StuffIt scripting commands, syntax, and arguments, along with brief examples of how to use them to build your scripts.

The **Appendix, Common Questions (and Answers!),** answers some of your questions that might come up when you use the software.

The **Index** helps you navigate through this User's Guide.

Manual Conventions

This manual assumes that you know how to operate the Macintosh and are familiar with basic Macintosh terminology such as point, click, drag, and the Finder. If you aren't familiar with these terms, you should refer to the Macintosh User's Guide to learn the basic operations of using the Macintosh.

In addition, several conventions are used throughout this User's Guide:

• Numbered items are steps that you must follow to complete a procedure.

• Alternate methods for completing a procedure are marked with a square.

• When referring to scripts, all commands are in a `typewriter font.`

Note: Text that appears between lines like this contains additional information that may be of use to some users.

Now that we've told you a bit about this User's Guide, let's get started learning about the software!

A Primer

Introduction

The StuffIt Deluxe application does four main things to your files and folders:

• it lets you combine files and folders in compressed files called archives and later manipulate the contents of archives,

• it lets you protect them from unauthorized viewing and editing with its security features, and

• it lets you translate foreign file formats into a form that can be used on a Macintosh.

SpaceSaver, a control panel in your StuffIt Deluxe package, operates independently of the StuffIt application and does three main things:

• it compresses files (individually and within folders),

• it can be set to work in the background, automatically compressing files older than a time frame you specify, and

• it lets you combine files and folders in compressed archives.

Compression: Saving Space on Disk

What is compression?

Compression is the process by which a file or a folder is made smaller. Software that compresses files can use any set of methods, called algorithms, by which the sequences of characters that make up a file are analyzed and reorganized in a more efficient manner, thereby saving space on disk. Compression algorithms vary widely from program to program and the usual trade-off among algorithms is between speed and degree of compression. If an algorithm compresses quickly, it will not be able to compress as well as one that spends additional time improving its compression.

StuffIt Deluxe and SpaceSaver strike the best balance between the fastest compression methods (which compress less) and those that save the most space (which take more time).

Though there are many uses for compression technologies, the three primary purposes are to save disk space, to speed modem and network transfers, and to save space when doing a backup.

Archiving: The Basics of Combining Files and Folders

What is an archive?

An archive is a special document that can contain more than a single file or folder. Archiving is the process by which one or more files and folders are combined into a single document and often compressed during the process. StuffIt archives are those archives created by any member of the StuffIt family of products.

There are three advantages to storing documents in an archive:

• Archives usually contain compressed files, and thereby save space on disk and reduce the time it takes to transmit them over phone lines or networks.

• Files stored in an archive can be sent over networks and telecommunication lines as a single document making it easier for other people to retrieve all related material.

• Associated files can be kept in one archive for easy retrieval and backup.

With this software, you can create a special type of archive called a "self-extracting archive." A self-extracting archive is an archive that can be decompressed by anyone – even if the recipient doesn't own SpaceSaver or another compression product.

Security: Protecting Files from Others

What is security?

Security is a means by which files are secured from prying eyes. StuffIt provides security for your files using two methods in conjunction with one another:

• encryption, which scrambles the data according to certain standards for encrypting files;

• a password, which ensures that only users who know the password can access the files in an archive.

SpaceSaver Defined

What is SpaceSaver?

SpaceSaver is compression software for saving space on disks. The flexible design of SpaceSaver allows you to accomplish the goal of saving disk space in a number of ways. SpaceSaver allows you to individually, or manually, save disk space on command, or automatically save space while your computer is not being used. The best part of using SpaceSaver is that you can continue to use your Macintosh normally. When you open a file, SpaceSaver transparently expands it and, when you save, SpaceSaver compresses it again—without any effort on your part.

Manual compression can be easily done by either attaching a specified keyword–a prefix or suffix added to the name of your file, folder or disk names—or by using a menu command. You can compress anything by simply clicking on its icon and choosing a menu item from Magic Menu (our extension to the Finder) or just by changing its Finder Label. Either way, SpaceSaver compresses it right on the spot, saving an average of 50% of the original disk space used by the file.

SpaceSaver's automatic compression will compress files when your computer is not being used. With Idle Time Compression, you can set SpaceSaver to compress files that haven't been modified for a certain amount of time. Since SpaceSaver works while the machine is inactive, you always maximize the usage of your disk space.

Magic Menu Defined

What is Magic Menu?

An essential part of this package is the Magic Menu Finder Extension. Magic Menu is a menu that appears just after the Special menu in the Finder. With point-and-click simplicity, select any icon from the Finder and compress it by choosing a menu item from the Magic Menu.

Magic Menu is so useful that it is used with three major functions of this software. You can archive with it, compress files with it, and send electronic mail with it. Because it does so many things, you'll find information about each and every use it has in three different chapters.

StuffIt Deluxe Defined

What is StuffIt Deluxe?

The StuffIt Deluxe software provides compression, archiving, security, and the ability to translate and convert other compression and foreign file formats and more.

StuffIt Deluxe is comprised of

• StuffIt Deluxe, the application,

• the StuffIt Viewer Extensions,

• the StuffIt Network/Communications Extensions,

• the StuffIt Tools/Utilities, and

• the Automating StuffIt scripting language and tools.

In the future, more extensions will be added to StuffIt Deluxe.

StuffIt Deluxe's powerful compression methods save space on your storage devices, but the application goes beyond SpaceSaver's handling of archives because it provides you with many tools for managing and manipulating your archives. The key to StuffIt is its ability to move files in and out of archives, or from archive to archive, and it gives you everything you need to develop a strategy for everyday archiving. On top of these core abilities you can build additional ones with the StuffIt Extensions (explained in detail below).

The Extensions Defined

StuffIt Deluxe supports an open architecture where individual modules can be used to extend the functionality of the product. In all, the Extensions are best broken into four categories: Viewer Extensions, Network/ Communication Extensions, Tools/Utilities, and Automating StuffIt Tools.

What are the Viewer Extensions?

StuffIt Deluxe comes with viewers that let you view text and PICT files before UnStuffing them from archives. Text "Read Me" documents can be enclosed within StuffIt archives and are automatically viewed when opening an archive. They can be saved and printed as separate documents.

What are the Network/ Communication Extensions?

The world of compression extends outward from the user to local and remote networks, to other computer systems, and to online telecommunication services. The StuffIt Deluxe Network and Communication Extensions, translate files to and from other archive programs (such as PackIt, Zip, and Arc) and from other data formats commonly found on IBM PCs, Digital VAXen, and Unix machines.

But that's not all. StuffIt gives you hooks into the wide world of electronic mail. And if you're sending files via phone lines, you can Stuff and UnStuff within telecommunication programs like MicroPhone II and White Knight.

What are the Tools/ Utilities?

This package includes a set of tools and utilities to help you accomplish certain tasks more easily.

What are Drop•Stuff and Drop•UnStuff?

Drop•Stuff and Drop•UnStuff extend the functionality of the Apple Finder for System 7 users. The Drop Boxes let you drag one or more items onto the "drop box" icons for easy Stuffing and UnStuffing.

What is StuffIt Converter?

StuffIt Converter batch converts Compact Pro archives, AppleLink packages, and archives Stuffed with older versions of StuffIt, improving the quality of their compression and enabling them to take advantage of the current features of StuffIt Deluxe.

What is StuffIt XTND?

StuffIt XTND is a Claris system extension that lets you hook StuffIt into programs such as On Location, a disk indexer from On Technology, or other software products that support XTNDs.

Automating StuffIt

StuffIt can be easily automated for routine tasks. Not only does this automation include a built-in scripting language, but StuffIt supports Apple events so that, when using System 7, other applications can communicate with StuffIt without any interaction on your part. We also provide several extensions to products like QuicKeys 2, HyperCard, and MPW that let you automate Stuffing and UnStuffing tasks with those packages.

How Do I Automate StuffIt?

Even our ready-made extensions don't provide all users with the kind of power they need, so we've provided a scripting language that lets you tailor-make your own StuffIt archival strategy.

Scripting StuffIt from Within.

You can write scripts that will automate actions that you do all the time, such as backing up and archiving your word processing files, or segmenting and making a backup of your database, or moving files from one archive to another. Building scripts with StuffIt's scripting language begins with a "watch me" feature that lets you record actions in real time. As the action is recorded, a script is automatically written for you. You can edit this script later and add this script to a menu so you can execute the script at any time with ease.

Automating StuffIt from Outside.

You can use the "Automating StuffIt Tools" to extend QuicKeys 2, HyperCard, or MPW for automation of Stuffing and UnStuffing tasks within those macro and scripting products. StuffIt Deluxe also supports a full set of Apple events, which allows other applications or scripting products, such as Userland Frontier, to "remote control" the StuffIt application when using System 7.

UnStuffIt Defined

What is UnStuffIt?

UnStuffIt is an application that allows you to decompress files that have been compressed with any StuffIt product including StuffIt Lite™ (our shareware utility), StuffIt Deluxe, and StuffIt SpaceSaver.

UnStuffIt is a freeware product, which means that you may give it away to your friends, family, or anyone you please, as long as you don't charge for it or distribute it with a commercial product. **It is the only part of this package that you may freely copy and give away.**

A Note About System 6 and System 7

StuffIt Deluxe works with both System 6 and System 7. There are certain features, however, that will not work with System 6 because they are specific to System 7 only. These include Balloon Help, special support of aliases, and

Apple events. Aladdin Systems went to great lengths to ensure that the use of the software with System 6 was not diminished.

This User's Guide focuses on System 7. Wherever functionality is different under System 6, you'll find notes describing System 6 usage.

Users of System 7 will be happy to know that the entire StuffIt Deluxe package is System 7-savvy, 32-bit clean, '040 cache compatible, and fully Apple event aware.

Balloon Help

We make it possible for you to get online assistance whenever you need it. Using System 7's Balloon Help, you'll find that help is available for menu commands and descriptions of the contents of dialogs. Balloon Help can be turned on and off from the Help menu in the upper right corner of your screen.

If you find that help balloons don't answer all your questions, you'll always find the answer here in the User's Guide. If you can't find an answer in this User's Guide, Technical Support is available via phone, fax, or E-Mail to answer your specific questions. See the inside cover for details.

Note: Balloon help is available only to System 7 users. System 6 users do not have online help.

Chapter 2: Installation

Requirements

StuffIt Deluxe operates on any Macintosh family computer provided you have at least two megabytes of memory. A hard drive is also required.

Though StuffIt Deluxe is compatible with System 6.0.5 or later, you should always use the latest System and Finder available from Apple Computer, Inc., provided by your local dealer. StuffIt Deluxe and SpaceSaver are fully compatible with System 7.

Easy Installation

Before you install StuffIt Deluxe, you should make a copy of your two StuffIt Deluxe diskettes, store the originals in a safe place, and use the copy to install StuffIt Deluxe on your hard disk. We also suggest that you take a few moments now to complete the registration card and send it to Aladdin Systems (it's postage paid). Follow the steps below to proceed with the Easy Installation.

1. Insert the StuffIt Deluxe Disk One into your Macintosh.

2. Locate the Installer icon on the disk and double-click it.

3. An informational dialog will appear; read it and then click "OK".

4. The Easy Installation dialog will now appear. Select the drive you wish to install StuffIt Deluxe onto using the "Switch Disk" button. Click the "Install" button to begin the installation process.

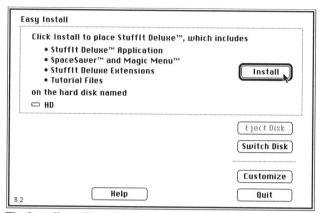

The Installer will put SpaceSaver and Magic Menu into your System folder for System 6, or the Control Panels folder for System 7. It will also create a folder called "StuffIt Deluxe Folder" which contains the StuffIt Deluxe application, Tutorial and Sample files, the StuffIt Tools & Utilities, the Network and Communications extensions, and a "Read Me" document that contains up-to-date information about our software.The installer will also place required files into other locations in your System Folder. We'll talk about these in detail later.

5. When Disk One is ejected, insert Disk Two as requested.

6. When the installation is finished, a dialog will appear telling you the installation is successful. Click the "Restart" button to complete the installation process.

As your Macintosh restarts, you'll see both the SpaceSaver and Magic Menu icons appear along the bottom of your screen.

The SpaceSaver startup icon

The Magic Menu startup icon

Note: If you are using an Extensions manager such as INITPicker™ (from Microseeds Publishing, Inc.), you may need to additionally configure it to include SpaceSaver and Magic Menu. Consult the Extension manager's manual for how this is done if you're not already familiar with the process.

Personalizing StuffIt SpaceSaver

Shortly after restarting, you'll see a dialog asking you to personalize your copy of the SpaceSaver software. The first time you use the StuffIt Deluxe application, you'll have to personalize it too.

The insertion point is already located in the Name field, so,

1. Type your name (for example, David Schargel) and press the tab key to enter the Company field.

2. Type the name of your company, if you have one (for example, Aladdin Systems, Inc.).

3. Click "OK" to have SpaceSaver permanently save this personal information.

When you are done personalizing the software, one immediate difference you'll find is that the Magic Menu appears immediately after the Special menu in the Finder's menu bar. Just for future reference, here is the Magic Menu.

Note: On some systems, the word "Magic" appears in the Finder's menu bar, instead of the Magic Menu icon shown in this manual.

You're now ready to use either SpaceSaver or Magic Menu. You might want to get started immediately by turning to "Chapter 3: Using StuffIt SpaceSaver," beginning on page 23, but we suggest that you at least continue the next 6 steps now to personalize the StuffIt Deluxe application.

Personalizing the StuffIt Deluxe Application

The StuffIt Deluxe application needs to be personalized independently of SpaceSaver. The first time you open the StuffIt Deluxe application, you'll be prompted to enter your name, company, and serial number, which can be found just inside this User's Guide.

1. Open the "StuffIt Deluxe Folder" that was created on your hard disk.

2. Double-click on the "StuffIt Deluxe™ 3.0" icon.

StuffIt Deluxe™ 3.0

StuffIt will open and a dialog will appear for you to personalize your software by entering your name, your company's name, and the serial number of your copy of StuffIt Deluxe.

The insertion point will already be located in the Name field, ready for you to type.

3. Type your name (for example, David Schargel) and press the tab key to enter the Company field.

4. Type the name of your company, if you have one (for example, Aladdin Systems, Inc.).

5. Type the Serial Number of your copy of StuffIt Deluxe.

You can find the serial number imprinted on the card just inside the cover of this User's Guide.

6. Click "OK" to have StuffIt Deluxe permanently save this information.

You're now ready to begin using the StuffIt Deluxe software! We suggest you start using the software by turning to page 23 where you'll find the beginning of "Chapter 3: Using StuffIt SpaceSaver." With the instructions there, you'll be up and running with the software in under 5 minutes.

Custom Installation

If you want to select the specific items to be installed follow the steps below. If you haven't done so already, you should make a copy of your StuffIt Deluxe Disk One and Two, store the originals in a safe place, and use the copies to install StuffIt Deluxe on your hard disk.

1. Insert the StuffIt Deluxe Disk One into your Macintosh.

2. Locate the Installer icon on the disk and double click on it.

3. An informational dialog will appear; read it and then click "OK".

The main installation dialog will now appear.

4. Select the drive you wish to install StuffIt Deluxe onto using the "Switch Disk" button.

5. Click the "Customize" button to begin selection for a Custom Install.

The custom installation dialog appears, with a list showing the groups of files available for installation.

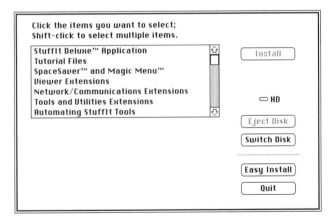

StuffIt Deluxe Application

This installs the StuffIt Deluxe™ application onto your hard disk, as well as Preference files and a "Read Me" file. These are the minimal files you'll need to use the application. See "Chapter 4: Using StuffIt Deluxe," beginning on page 45, for basic tutorials on using the StuffIt application.

Tutorial Files

This installs Tutorial files onto your hard disk. The Tutorial Files are used in "Chapter 4: Using StuffIt Deluxe."

SpaceSaver and Magic Menu

This option installs the StuffIt SpaceSaver and Magic Menu control panels onto your hard disk. Installing these control panels allows you to compress and decompress files from the Finder. The basics of using these two essential utilities are covered in "Chapter 3: Using StuffIt SpaceSaver" which starts on page 23.

Viewer Extensions

This option installs the files needed to allow you to view the contents of Text or PICT documents in StuffIt archives. See "Chapter 5: The Viewers Extensions," beginning on page 97, for use of Viewer "Read Me" files.

Network/Communication Extensions

This installs files for all the Networking and Communications features you can use with StuffIt. This includes the Translators, MicroPhone II scripts, and a Magic Menu Extension that provides support for Stuffing and Sending archives using QuickMail and Microsoft Mail. See "Chapter 6: Network/Communication Extensions," beginning on page 107, for tutorials on using these Extensions.

Tools/Utilities Extensions

This option installs miscellaneous utilities that will be useful when working with StuffIt archives. These include the StuffIt Converter, the Drop•Stuff and Drop•UnStuff Drop Boxes for use under System 7, and a Claris XTND file. See "Chapter 7: The Tools/Utilities," beginning on page 135, for use of these tools and utilities.

Automating StuffIt Tools

This option installs scripts which allow you to automate many of StuffIt's common tasks using StuffIt's built-in scripting language or other macro/scripting products such as CE Software's QuicKeys 2, Claris' Hypercard, and Apple Computer's MPW. See "Chapter 8: Automating StuffIt," beginning on page 151, for tutorials, or see the "Chapter 10: Scripting Reference," beginning on page 175, for details on the scripting language.

UnStuffIt

This option places the freeware program UnStuffIt on your hard disk. You can give it away to your friends, family, or anyone you please, as long as you don't charge for it or distribute it with a commercial product. It's installed as a self-extracting archive to make it easier for you give to others. **It is the only part of this package that you may freely copy and give away**. See "Chapter 9: UnStuffIt," beginning on page 171, for information on using UnStuffIt.

6. Scroll through the list of items and Shift-click the ones you want to install.

As you select items, their names appear at the lower-left portion of the dialog. If you select only a single item, detail about it appear.

7. Click "Install" to install the selected items.

8. If Disk One is ejected, insert Disk Two as requested.

9. When the installation is finished, a dialog will appear telling you the installation is successful. Click the "Restart" button to complete the installation process.

You should now turn to page 17 to begin the personalization process.

Where is StuffIt Deluxe Installed?

The StuffIt Installer places files and folders in two locations: The StuffIt Deluxe Folder and the System Folder.

Within the Extensions folder in your System Folder, a newly created "Aladdin" folder will contain StuffIt Deluxe's plug-in modules. Let's look at each folder.

The StuffIt Deluxe Folder

The StuffIt Deluxe Folder is a new folder created on your hard disk when you installed the software. It contains the StuffIt applications, as well as folders containing other tools and documents that you'll find useful. The other location where files are placed is your System Folder.

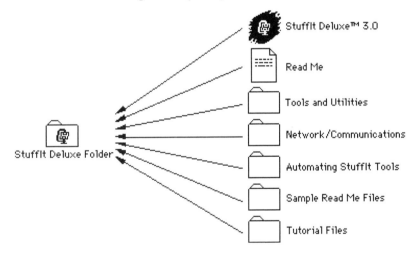

The System Folder

The System Folder will get the Extensions, Control Panels, and Preferences, automatically placed in the appropriate locations.

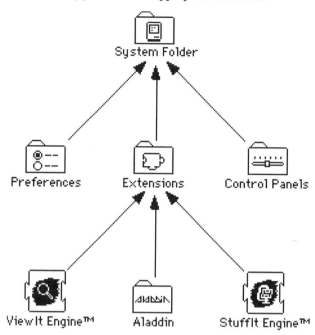

Note: If you are using System 6, the controlpanels will be placed inside your System Folder and not in the Control Panels folder.

The Aladdin Folder

Within your Extensions folder, you'll find a newly created folder, called the "Aladdin" folder. Here you'll find the plug-in modules that are used by the StuffIt application and Magic Menu.

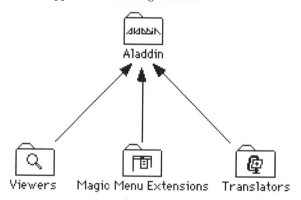

Where to Go

Now that the software is fully installed on your Macintosh, let's get down to basics. We start with the easy-to-use StuffIt SpaceSaver.

Chapter 3:
Using StuffIt SpaceSaver

Section One: Manual Compression

Ways to Save Space

As we mentioned in the Introduction, you can use SpaceSaver to save disk space selectively at your command or automatically while your computer is not being used.

This portion of the chapter, "Manual Compression," discusses how you can compress anything on demand. This can be done a few ways:

• by either attaching a 'keyword,' a prefix or suffix, to file or folder names,

• by using the Magic Menu, or

• with Finder Labels. The heading "Compress on Label," on page 37, discusses how to compress items with Labels.

The following sections in this chapter show you other ways to save disk space and how to customize SpaceSaver and Magic Menu to fit your working style.

Example: Compressing Folders

Feature Explained: Keyword compression.

Related Topics: See the tutorial "Example: Compressing Individual Files," beginning on page 25, and how to change the keyword preference item, "Compress on Keyword" on page 36.

Problem: You've been working with your Macintosh for a while, and you've created a lot of files in your "Documents Folder" to the point that you've almost run out of disk space. What do you do?

Solution: You attach the SpaceSaver keyword to your "Documents Folder", creating a "Small Documents Folder" in three easy steps.

1. **Select the folder you want to compress by clicking on its name in the Finder. The name of the folder will now be ready for editing.**

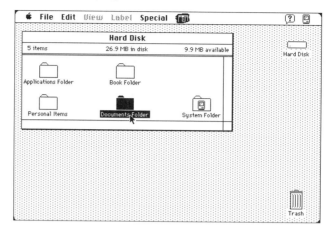

2. **Position the insertion point at the beginning of the name and type the preconfigured keyword, "Small".**

Notes: The SpaceSaver keyword can be attached to the beginning or end of a folder name. In this example we use it at the start of the folder name.

Instead of using the word "small", the SpaceSaver keyword can be configured to your liking. This is discussed in "Compress on Keyword" on page 36.

---

3. **Click in the white space outside the icon.**

As SpaceSaver compresses the folder, a spinning StuffIt cursor will indicate that SpaceSaver is hard at work. When the cursor returns to an arrow, you'll know that SpaceSaver has completed its task.

Note: This spinning StuffIt cursor is the default progress indicator. It's also possible to instruct SpaceSaver to display full progress dialogs or no progress indicator at all. These preferences are explained later in "Status Display" on page 34.

You can now use these compressed files as you did before you compressed them. Double-clicking them in the Finder will open them as it did before, as will opening them directly from an application – SpaceSaver automatically decompresses the file. When you complete working on the file and close it, SpaceSaver will recompress it.

Alternate Methods

- SpaceSaver will compress or decompress any file or folder when you drag it into or out of a "small" folder. This can be very useful for saving disk space without renaming anything. Drag items into a common "small" folder.

- You can Save a file into a "small" folder. SpaceSaver will automatically compress it.

- You can select any file or folder and choose "Compress" from the Magic Menu in the Finder.

Note: Any folder, except your System Folder, can be compressed with SpaceSaver or Magic Menu.

Example: Compressing Individual Files

Feature Explained: Compressing within an application.

Related Topic: See the heading, "Compress on Keyword" on page 36 for details on how to change the compression keyword.

Problem: You're working on a presentation and the file has grown so large that you want to save it into a compressed form from within your current application.

Solution: When using the "Save As…" command from the application, attach the SpaceSaver keyword to the name of the file and it will be compressed as it is saved.

1. Choose "Save As…" from the application's File menu.

2. Add the SpaceSaver keyword to the file's name.

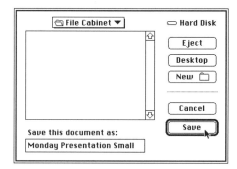

3. Select the destination for the saved document and click "Save".

As SpaceSaver compresses the file, a spinning StuffIt cursor will indicate that SpaceSaver is working. When the cursor returns to its previous state, you'll know that SpaceSaver has completed its task. On smaller files, compression will happen so quickly that you may not even notice the cursor.

Alternate Method

■ Save the file into a folder or disk that is already designated as "small".

Example: Sending a Folder to a Friend

Feature Explained: self-extracting archives.

Related Topics: If you're creating self-extracting archives from Magic Menu, see "Make Self-Extracting Preferences" on page 43. If you're creating self-extracting archives from the StuffIt Deluxe application, see the tutorial "Example: Self-Extracting Archives," beginning on page 67, in "Chapter 4: Using StuffIt Deluxe."

Problem: You're collaborating with a fellow author on a book and you want to send her the first four chapters via modem. Each chapter is its own file and each file has grown rather large. You'd like to compress them all before you send them, and you'd like to send them all as one archive to her, but she doesn't own any StuffIt software. What do you do?

Solution: Attach the ".sea" keyword to the folder to create a self-extracting archive.

1. Place all the files you'd like to send to her in a single folder (if they're not already organized that way).

Book Folder

2. From the Finder, attach the reserved keyword ".sea" to the end of the folder name.

3. Click on a blank space elsewhere in the Finder (or press Return).

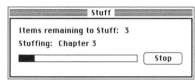

As SpaceSaver compresses the folder, a progress dialog will indicate that SpaceSaver is hard at work. When the progress dialog indicates that it's done, you'll know that SpaceSaver has completed its task.

You can now send the self-extracting archive to your friend.

Book Folder .sea

Your friend can expand the file simply by double-clicking on it. A dialog will ask her where the expanded folder should be placed.

As your folder is expanding, a progress dialog comes up, showing how the expansion is proceeding. When the process is finished, your friend is ready to use the files in the folder. That's all there is to it!

Note: If your friend now tries to re-attach the ".sea" keyword to the expanded folder to recompress it, she won't be able to because she doesn't own StuffIt SpaceSaver. There's only one solution for that—she can buy her own copy!

Alternate Methods

■ By using the ".sit" keyword, you can create a StuffIt archive. These are smaller than self-extracting archives, but require the recipient to have a StuffIt product to UnStuff them.

■ The ".sit" or ".sea" keywords can also be appended to individual files.

■ Select one or more icons and select "Stuff" (Command-S) or "Make Self-Extracting" from the Magic Menu to create a ".sit" or ".sea" file, respectively.

Example: Expanding Multiple Items

Feature Explained: Magic Menu Expand.

Related Topics: See "Magic Menu Compression Preferences," beginning on page 40, and "Hooking up with the Finder and Magic Menu" in "Chapter 7: The Tools/Utilities" for more information.

Problem: After downloading a number of files from an online service, you want to UnStuff all of them at once. SpaceSaver requires you to remove the ".sit" suffix from each archive one by one. Is there an easier way?

Solution: Use the Magic Menu to solve this problem in one fell swoop.

1. Select one or more items from the Finder.

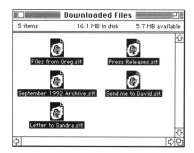

2. Choose "Expand" (Command-U) from the Magic Menu.

Magic Menu will UnStuff the files from each archive. If any archive contains more than one item, a new folder will be created (for each archive) and the contents will be UnStuffed into that folder.

Note: The Expand command in Magic Menu is preconfigured to expand SpaceSaver files, StuffIt archives (.sit or .sea), Compact Pro™ archives (.cpt), and AppleLink™ packages (.PKG) using this method.

Section Two: Automatic Compression

Idle Time Compression

Idle Time Compression™, a powerful feature of SpaceSaver, runs an automatic compression process whenever your Macintosh is on but not in use, in much the same way a screensaver does.

You can set the Idle Time Compression preferences to compress files that have not been modified for a specified amount of time. When files age past that amount of time, they're automatically compressed.

If SpaceSaver is in the process of compressing a file when you move the mouse or hit a key, SpaceSaver will immediately give you back the control of your computer. It will resume Idle Time Compression only when your computer is again idle for the specified amount of time.

Note: If a Macintosh Portable or PowerBook is running off battery power, Idle Time Compression will not run in the background. This is done to prevent the draining of the battery. Once the computer is plugged in, the automatic compression features of SpaceSaver will be active again.

Example: Automatically Compressing Your Hard Disk

Feature Explained: Idle Time Compression.

Related Topic: See the heading, "Compress on Keyword," on page 36, on how to change the compression keyword.

Problem: You are running out of disk space and you don't want to manually compress items on your hard disk. You just want SpaceSaver to maximize your available space. How do you do that?

Solution: Use the Idle Time compression feature and let SpaceSaver do the compression for you when you are not around. First, you must turn on Idle Time Compression from the control panel.

1. Pull down the Apple menu and choose "Control Panels".

2. Locate and double click the SpaceSaver icon.

Note: This step guides you using System 7. If you are using System 6, you should now locate SpaceSaver in the scrolling list and click on its icon.

3. When the SpaceSaver control panel appears, click the "Idle Time..." button (at the bottom of the control panel.)

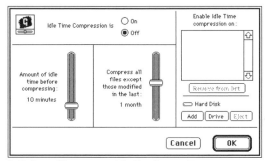

A dialog will appear with the four options you can set for the Idle Time Compression process.

"Idle Time Compression is On/Off" lets you turn this feature on and off. "Amount of idle time before compressing:" is a slider bar where you can set the amount of time your computer is idle before SpaceSaver will begin compressing files. "Compress all files except those modified in the last:" is another slider bar that allows you to set how old files need to be before they're compressed. The "Enable Idle Time Compression on:" option lets you add or remove disk names from a list of those disks targeted for Idle Time Compression.

4. Click on the "On" button. A dialog will appear asking you whether you want to turn on Idle Time Compression or not. Click "Yes".

5. Set the amount of idle time after which Idle Time compression will activate using the "Amount of Idle Time before compressing?" slider. If you are happy with the default time of 10 minutes, skip to the next step.

This setting can be set in fixed increments from 1 to 60 minutes.

Note: This slider also indicates the amount of time to wait before the "Postpone recompression until the machine is idle" option activates to recompress files. You can find details in "Postpone Recompression Until the Machine is Idle" on page 35.

6. Set the amount of time that files must have aged (since the last time they were saved or modified) using the "Compress all files except those modified in the last:" slider. If you like the default time of 1 month, skip to the next step.

This slider setting can be set in fixed increments from 1 day to 1 year.

7. Add one or more disks to the "Enable Idle Time Compression on:" list by selecting the disk(s) you want by clicking the "Drive" button until the disk's name appears, then click the "Add" button to add it to your list.

The name of the disk will now appear in the "Enable Idle Time Compression on:" list. It is important that you add disks to this list so that SpaceSaver knows which disks to work on during Idle Time Compression. We leave the choice of which disks you want compressed since you might have removable disks, diskettes, or file servers that you wouldn't want Idle Time Compression run on.

You can later use the "Remove from list" button to remove disks from the list of those targeted for Idle Time Compression.

8. Click "OK".

Idle Time Compression is now activated on the volumes you've chosen and compression will begin when your computer has been idle for the specified amount of time.

Note: You can always specify individual files or folders that you never want SpaceSaver to compress. This can either be done with a "big" keyword or a specified Finder label. See "Identifying Items Never to Compress," on page 38, to learn how to do this.

If you leave your Macintosh on overnight, you will return to see a large amount of disk space available on your hard disk. Now you know why we call it SpaceSaver!

Section Three: Mastering SpaceSaver and Magic Menu

Preferences

We mentioned that SpaceSaver was designed with flexibility in mind. There are preferences that help you use SpaceSaver and Magic Menu better. SpaceSaver preferences are set through the SpaceSaver control panel while Magic Menu preferences are set with a command in the Magic Menu. Preferences for the StuffIt Deluxe application are set using the "Preferences…" command from StuffIt's Edit menu. See "Close-up: Setting Your Preferences," beginning on page 84, for setting the StuffIt Deluxe preferences.

When talking about the SpaceSaver control panel preferences, this section only reviews the general preferences of the SpaceSaver control panel. The "Idle Time," or automatic compression preferences are not discussed here, but rather in "Section Two: Automatic Compression" that starts on page 28.

The SpaceSaver Control Panel

Feature Explained: SpaceSaver control panel.

Related Topic: The "Idle Time," or automatic compression preferences are discussed in "Section Two: Automatic Compression" that starts on page 28.

When you installed the software, certain preferences were preset to make it easier for you to get up and running. You can change these preferences to customize SpaceSaver to your liking. To change your preferences, you need to access the SpaceSaver control panel.

1. Pull down the Apple menu and choose "Control Panels".

2. Locate and double-click the SpaceSaver icon.

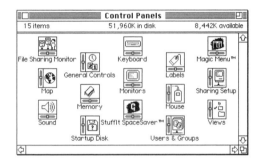

Note: This example guides you using System 7. If you are using System 6, you should now locate SpaceSaver in the scrolling list and click on its icon.

Control Panel General Preferences

SpaceSaver On/Off

The most important preference is whether SpaceSaver is On or Off. Unless you want to disable SpaceSaver, leave the "On" button selected.

Status Display

Immediately to the right of the On and Off buttons are the "Status display" buttons for selecting which progress indicator to use. This indicator comes up whenever you compress or decompress with SpaceSaver. You have three choices: a progress dialog, an animated StuffIt cursor, or none.

Progress Dialog

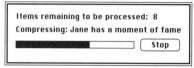

This is the progress dialog status bar for showing the progress of an item being compressed or decompressed. Although this option will slow down SpaceSaver a bit, it is the most informative of the progress indicators because graphically shows how much has been completed and how much remains to be completed. The progress dialog will not appear until a few seconds after the process has begun.

Animated StuffIt Cursor

This is the animated StuffIt cursor whose watch spins when you're compressing or decompressing any item. It is the default setting when you install the software. This option is useful for quietly telling you when SpaceSaver is working.

None

No SpaceSaver progress indicator will be displayed when you compress or decompress an item.

Verify Writes

Below the On/Off buttons is the "Verify writes" check box. Checking this preference turns on file verification for reading and writing. This verification will double check that the file written during a compression or expansion operation is precisely the same file that was read from disk. If the file is not identical, an error dialog will appear telling you that the file could not be verified. Turning this preference on increases the amount of time it takes to compress or decompress a file.

The default setting for "Verify writes" is off. In most cases it is not necessary to use "Verify writes", unless you're concerned about the reliability of one or more of your hard disks.

Control Panel Compression Preferences

Below the "Verify writes" check box you'll find the "Compression…" button. Click this button to see a dialog that allows you to set preferences such as Compression methods and other ways to optimize your use of SpaceSaver. We also present a way for you to identify items that should never be compressed.

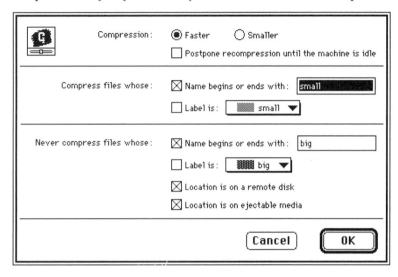

Compression

The top grouping of options allows you to tell SpaceSaver how you want compression to be performed. In addition to identifying whether you want SpaceSaver to emphasize speed or size, you can instruct SpaceSaver to postpone recompressing your files so it will never interfere with your work.

Faster

Selecting the "Faster" button means that files will be compressed as rapidly as possible.

Smaller

Selecting the "Smaller" button means that files will be made as small as possible. Selecting "Smallest" slightly increases the time it takes to compress files, but expansion will always be lightning fast.

Postpone Recompression Until the Machine is Idle

The "Postpone recompression until the machine is idle" option allows you to specify whether SpaceSaver should recompress files immediately upon their being closed or wait until your computer is inactive to recompress them. If you don't want to see the slight delay of files being recompressed, then check this box. See "Section Two: Automatic Compression," beginning on page 28, for information on setting the amount of idle time before your files will be recompressed.

Identifying Items to Compress

SpaceSaver allows you to define your own keyword or label that identifies an item to be compressed. The "Compress files whose:" portion of the Compression Preferences dialog lets you customize these features.

Compress on Keyword

SpaceSaver doesn't have to use the preset keyword "small". You can set almost any keyword you want by changing the text after "Name begins or ends with:". Once changed, attaching this new keyword to any file, folder, or disk name will compress that file. The Compression Preferences also allows you to turn off keyword use by unchecking the "Compress files whose: Name begins or ends with:" option.

Follow these easy steps to change a keyword to your liking.

1. If you're not already in the "Compression Preferences" dialog, go to the SpaceSaver control panel and click on the "Compression…" button.

2. Type your new keyword where it says "Compress files whose: Name begins or ends with:".

3. Click "OK" in this dialog and close the SpaceSaver control panel.

Now anytime you use that new "Compress" keyword, SpaceSaver will know to compress that item.

After you set a new "Compress" keyword, everything that had the old keyword will stay compressed. The next time these items are decompressed, they will remain expanded and will not be recompressed.

Note: A keyword can consist of between one and fifteen alphanumeric characters (letters, numbers, punctuation marks or anything you can type on the keyboard), though it is recommended that you keep it short. Some alternative keywords you might want to use are "*", "<" or "•". One character you cannot use is a colon (":").

Note: There are two "reserved keywords" that cannot be used. These are reserved for creating archives:
- ".sit" keywords are reserved for StuffIt archives.
- ".sea" keywords are reserved for self-extracting archives.

Compress on Label

An alternate way to compress files beyond keywords and the Magic Menu is to use Finder labels. The Macintosh Finder allows you to apply a label to any file, folder, or disk. To use labels, first you need to turn on this feature and then set the label you want to compress items with.

Note: This feature is unavailable for System 6 users.

1. If you're not already there, go to the SpaceSaver control panel and click on the "Compression…" button.

2. Check the "Compress files whose: Label is:" so that this check box is on.

3. Use the Label menu to choose the label you want to use for compression.

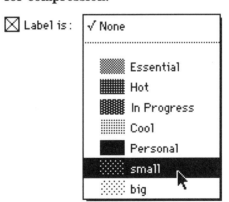

4. Click "OK" to this dialog and close the SpaceSaver control panel.

Anytime you want to use this feature, simply select an icon from the Finder and choose the label you designated from the Label menu. Shortly after a label is applied to an item, it will be compressed.

Note: System 7 users can change the color and/or the name of each label. This is done with the Labels control panel. See the Macintosh Owners Manual on how to accomplish this. You might want to use this System 7 feature to your advantage by changing a label name to "small" and coloring it so you can quickly identify it by sight.

Identifying Items Never to Compress

Just as you have a few ways to identify items to compress, SpaceSaver lets you define your own keyword or label that signifies an item should never be compressed. You can also have SpaceSaver never compress files on remote disks (like file servers or AppleTalk Remote Access disks) or on ejectable media such as diskettes or removable hard disk cartridges.

The ability to select individual items to never compress is a powerful one. For example, you can identify any folders to never be compressed and SpaceSaver will never touch them. It doesn't matter if this folder is within a small folder or if you're using idle time compression on the hard disk.

The "Never compress files whose:" portion of the Compression Preferences dialog lets you customize these options.

```
Never compress files whose :    ☒ Name begins or ends with :   [ big          ]
                                 ☐ Label is :   [ None  ▼ ]
                                 ☒ Location is on a remote disk
                                 ☒ Location is on ejectable media
```

Never Compress on Keyword

Attaching the preset "big" keyword to something tells SpaceSaver to never compress that item. Like all keywords, the word "big" can be at the beginning or end of the file, folder, or disk name. If a "big" item gets placed into a "small" folder, SpaceSaver will still not compress that item.

The Compression Preferences also allow you to turn off the "Never compress" keyword use by unchecking the "Never compress files whose: Name begins or ends with:" check box.

More importantly, you can also opt to give SpaceSaver your own "Never compress" keyword. This is easily done as follows.

1. If you're not already in the "Compression Preferences" dialog, go to the SpaceSaver control panel and click on the "Compression…" button.

2. Type your new keyword where it says "Never compress files whose: Name begins or ends with:".

3. Click "OK" to this dialog and close the SpaceSaver control panel.

Now anytime you use that new "Never compress" keyword, SpaceSaver will know not to compress the item to which it's applied.

Never Compress on Label

An alternate way to specify items that should never be compressed is to use Finder labels. To use a "Never compress label", you first need to turn on this feature and set the label you want to compress items with.

Note: This feature is not available for System 6 users.

---

1. If you're not already there, go to the SpaceSaver control panel and click on the "Compression..." button.

2. Check the "Never compress files whose: Label is:" so that this option is on.

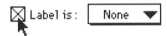

3. Use the Label menu to select the label you want to use.

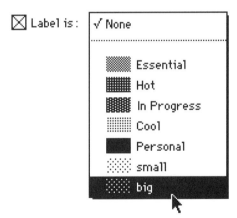

4. Click "OK" in this dialog and close the SpaceSaver control panel.

Anytime you want to use this feature, simply select an icon from the Finder and choose the label you designated from the Label menu.

Note: Selecting a "Never compress" label automatically expands the items that are already compressed.

Never Compress on Location   SpaceSaver comes preconfigured to never compress files on remote disks (like file servers and AppleTalk Remote Access disks) or on ejectable media such as diskettes or removable hard disk cartridges. This configuration was done for convenience—SpaceSaver can and does work on remote disks and ejectable media.

Location is on a Remote Disk   The "Location is on a remote disk" check box prevents you from creating or copying compressed files to shared disks, file servers, or disks made available using AppleTalk Remote Access or similar products. You might want to have this check box off if you want to have a "SpaceSaver Server," where everyone in your network has their own copy of SpaceSaver and wishes to access compressed files residing on a server.

Location is on Ejectable Media   The "Location is on ejectable media" check box prevents you from making or copying compressed files to disks that can be transported from location to location. The most common example of this are diskettes. SyQuest, Benoulli or other removable hard disks are also considered ejectable media. By unchecking this option, you allow for these types of disks to contain compressed files.

Idle Time Compression Preferences

To the right of the "Compression…" button in the SpaceSaver control panel, is the "Idle Time…" button. When you click this button, you'll be able to set all Idle Time Compression options. Since the Idle Time preferences are used when you use Idle Time Compression for the first time, the preferences are not discussed here but rather in the tutorials in "Section Two: Automatic Compression" that starts on page 28.

Magic Menu Compression Preferences

Features Explained: Magic Menu Compression Preferences.

Related Topics: See "Hooking up with the Finder and Magic Menu," beginning on page 137, in "Chapter 7: The Tools/Utilities" and, for information on using Magic Menu's "Mail", "Stuff and Mail", and "Mail Preferences…" commands, see "Section Two: Magic Menu and Electronic Mail," beginning on page 124, in "Chapter 6: Network/Communication Extensions."

When you installed the software, some basic Magic Menu preferences were preconfigured to make compression and expansion with Magic Menu effortless. You can change these preferences to better use the Magic Menu commands that are available to you. These preferences can be found in the

Finder by choosing "Preferences…" (found just under the "Make Self-Extracting" command) from the Magic Menu.

After choosing "Preferences…", you'll see the Magic Menu Compression Extension Preferences dialog.

Expand Preferences

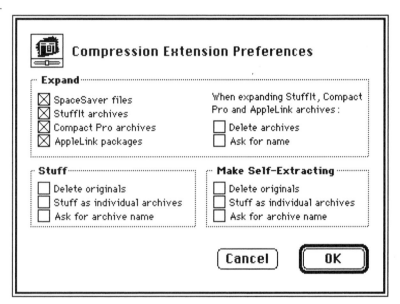

There are a few preferences that specifically address what happens when you expand any type of file from the Magic Menu.

SpaceSaver Files

The "SpaceSaver files" check box enables Magic Menu to expand, or decompress, files that have been compressed with StuffIt SpaceSaver. You may choose to turn this option off if you do not want Magic Menu's "Expand" command to work on "small" files. This option is checked on initial installation.

StuffIt Archives

If you have the "StuffIt archives" option checked, Magic Menu will expand, or UnStuff, any StuffIt archives when choosing "Expand" from the Magic Menu. StuffIt files are archives that are recognizable because they usually have ".sit" at the end of the file name. You might want to turn off this option if you want the "Expand" command to not UnStuff StuffIt archives. This option is checked on initial installation.

Compact Pro Archives

The "Compact Pro archives" check box does the same as the "StuffIt archives" check box, but it expands Compact Pro archives instead. Compact Pro is an archiving software product. A Compact Pro archive is identifiable by an file name that usually ends with ".cpt". The default for this check box is on.

AppleLink Packages

The "AppleLink packages" check box does the same as the "StuffIt archives" check box, but it expands AppleLink archives, which are usually called packages. AppleLink is Apple Computer Inc.'s telecommunications software that can create archives, or packages. An AppleLink package is identifiable by an file name that usually ends with ".PKG". The default for this check box is on.

Delete Archives

The "Delete archives" check box tells Magic Menu to delete the original archives just after they're expanded. This is very useful for clearing archives off your disk when the expanded software is ready for your use. This check box is preconfigured as off.

Ask For Name

The "Ask for name" check box lets Magic Menu bring up the standard Macintosh directory dialog for each archive to be expanded. When this dialog appears, you can change the name of files being extracted or save them to a different folder or disk. This check box is not checked when the software is installed.

Stuff Preferences

The Stuff options in the Preferences dialog lets you set the functionality for the Magic Menu "Stuff" command. Using the Stuff command is just like attaching ".sit" to a file or folder name except that with Magic Menu, you can select a number of files or folders to be Stuffed.

Delete Originals

Using the "Delete originals" check box will have Magic Menu delete all original files after they're placed into archives. This check box defaults off.

Stuff As Individual Archives

If you check the "Stuff as individual archives" option, Magic Menu will place every selected item into a multiple archives when Stuffing. If this check box is off, as it is preconfigured, whatever's selected when you choose "Stuff" will be combined into a one archive.

Ask For Archive Name

The "Ask for archive name" is a simple, self-explanatory check box. Turning it on has Magic Menu ask you for the name of the new archive, instead of automatically naming it. With this option checked, a directory dialog will appear so that you can save new archives in any folder or disk you want. This check box is not checked when SpaceSaver and Magic Menu are installed.

Note: The default name of an archive that contains multiple items is "Archive.sit". Using Magic Menu's "Stuff" command on a single item will create an archive using that item's name. If you'll be Stuffing often, you might want to set the "Ask for archive name" preference so that you always have an opportunity to name the new archives.

Make Self-Extracting Preferences

The "Make Self-Extracting" command in Magic Menu turns any selection into a double-clickable application. It's the same as attaching ".sea" to any file or folder name and is most useful for sending files to people who don't own any StuffIt software. The "Make Self-Extracting" options in the Preferences dialog sets the functionality for the Magic Menu "Make Self-Extracting" command.

Delete Originals

Using the "Delete originals" check box will have Magic Menu erase all original files after they're placed into a self-extracting archive. This check box is not checked by default.

Stuff As Individual Archives

If you check the "Stuff as individual archives" check box, you'll have Magic Menu place every selected item into multiple self-extracting archives. If this check box is off, as it is preconfigured, whatever is selected when you choose "Stuff" will be placed into a single self-extracting archive.

Ask For Archive Name

The "Ask for archive name" option forces Magic Menu to ask you for the name of the new archive, instead of automatically naming it. With this option checked, you can also automatically save the archive in any folder or disk you want. This option is not checked when the software is first installed.

Note: The default name of an self-extracting archive that contains multiple items is "Archive.sea". Using Magic Menu's "Make Self-Extracting" command on a single item will create an self-extracting archive using that item's name. If you'll be making self-extracting archives that contain multiple items on a regular basis, you might want to set the "Ask for archive name" check box so that you always have an opportunity to name new self-extracting archives.

Where to Go From Here

This completes the chapter on using StuffIt SpaceSaver. If you plan on stopping now, we suggest that turn on Idle Time Compression (if you haven't do so already) and leave your machine on overnight. This way, you'll find more disk space in the morning. If you want to continue, we recommend going on to the next part of the User's Guide, "Chapter 4: Using StuffIt Deluxe," where you'll learn about the StuffIt application.

Chapter 4:
Using StuffIt Deluxe

Section One: The Basics of StuffIt

Introduction

If you're not familiar with StuffIt, you should go through the examples given here to learn the basics of the program. If you're already familiar with StuffIt, you may want to skip right through the "The Basics of StuffIt" section and go to "Section Two: Beyond the Basics" and "Section Three: Mastering StuffIt Deluxe" in this chapter, or on to the "power user" chapters, 5 through 8. Since we've added some new features to StuffIt, however, even old-time StuffIt users might want to skim through this chapter. The examples given here may give you new ideas about saving space, archiving files, and securing your data. We move from the simplest problems and solutions to the most complex, covering all the main features of the program as we proceed.

Example: Stuffing a File

Features Explained: New Archive, Create 1.5.1 Archive, Archive Palette, Stuff, and Verify.

Related Topics: See "Close-up: The Archive Palette and Window" starting on page 70 and "Close-up: The Add Match Dialog," beginning on page 81, both in this chapter.

Problem: You're working on a desktop publishing project and you're adding text and graphics to a page layout file. You want to take the file home to work on it further, but it's over 900K, too big for a regular floppy. What do you do?

Solution: Use StuffIt to Stuff the file into an archive.

Creating a new archive and placing files into it is very simple. For the purposes of this tutorial, we've provided a small sample document called "A Document".

1. **If you're not in StuffIt, open the "StuffIt Deluxe Folder" in the Finder and launch the program now by double-clicking its icon.**

StuffIt Deluxe™ 3.0

StuffIt will launch and a floating window called the Archive Palette (shown here) will appear on your desktop with all of the buttons dimmed.

When the buttons are active, clicking them is equivalent to choosing their commands from the Archive menu. For now, leave the Archive Palette where it is.

2. **Choose "New…" (Command-N) from the File menu.**

StuffIt requires you to name an archive before you can work with it. Any time you choose "New…", a dialog appears with the default name "Archive.sit" and the prefix "Archive" selected.

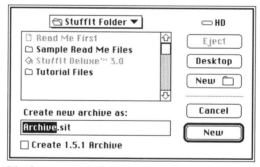

It's always a good idea to rename the initial "Archive" prefix to something more descriptive of an archive's contents.

3. **Type "Document" for the name of our tutorial archive.**

Note: You have the option to create this archive as a "1.5.1" archive by checking the "Create 1.5.1 Archive" check box. This is the version number for an older StuffIt format. 1.5.1 archives don't perform as well as version 3 archives, but we've provided the option for backward compatibility with older versions. Do not check this check box unless you wish to create a 1.5.1 archive.

---

4. Click the "New" button and StuffIt creates the empty archive "Document.sit" on disk.

A new archive window appears above the Archive Palette.

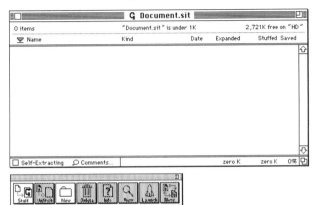

Notice how the Archive Palette has two active icons now: the "Stuff" icon for Stuffing files and folders into the archive, and the "New" folder icon, for creating new folders inside the archive.

5. Click the "Stuff" icon in the Archive Palette or choose "Stuff…" (Command-S) from the Archive menu.

A dialog appears with a directory listing on the left side containing a list of files and folders you can select from. This left part works like the "Open" dialog in most applications.

Note: Every icon on the Archive Palette has a corresponding menu command (and keyboard command key equivalent) in the Archive menu.

6. Enter the "Tutorial Files" folder, select the file called "A Document", and click the "Add" button.

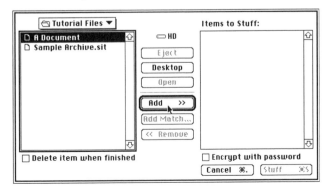

"A Document" will move to the "Items to Stuff" list on the right and the "Stuff" button (Command-S) will become active. You can add more files to our list, but don't do that now. If you've added the wrong file, simply select it in the "Items to Stuff" list and click the "Remove" button. StuffIt will remove the file and you can repeat the "Add" procedure, this time adding the correct file to the list of "Items to Stuff." Ignore the other options in this window for the moment.

7. Click the "Stuff" (Command-S) button.

A progress dialog appears showing StuffIt's progress as it Stuffs the file. If you want to cancel the operation, you can click the "Stop" button (or type Command-period at any time).

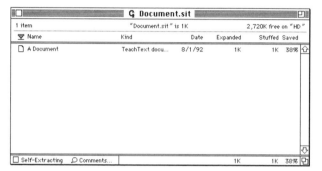

8. When the file is finished Stuffing, you can choose "Verify" (Command-Y) in the File menu to verify the integrity of the archive.

Verification is the process of ensuring that a file is exactly the same in an archive as it is on disk.

A progress dialog will appear, indicating that the contents of the archive are being verified. When verification is finished, you'll be informed of the results.

Note: The Macintosh normally verifies files as they are being read from or written to disk. This way, the Macintosh normally guarantees that you will never lose any information. The "Verify" command is not required each time you use StuffIt. You can verify any open archive, at anytime. We use it here to illustrate use of the command.

As a safeguard, SpaceSaver and the StuffIt application have two other related ways of verifying files. The ability to once again verify anything that is written to disk is provided as an option in the SpaceSaver Control Panel (see "Verify Writes" on page 34 of "Chapter 3: Using StuffIt SpaceSaver") and the Preferences dialog within the StuffIt application (see "Verify Writes" on page 86 in this chapter).

9. Click "OK".

That's it. You've just created your first archive and Stuffed a document into it.

This is a key operation within StuffIt Deluxe, though StuffIt has many other powerful features to be explored. We'll be taking a closer look at some of these at the end of this chapter, but for now, let's learn some more basics by completing another example. This time, we'll UnStuff a file, learning something about "Read Me" files as we go.

Alternate Methods

■ When the Stuff dialog opens, you have four ways to add files to an archive:

1. You can select files individually and add them to the "Items to Stuff" list by clicking the "Add" button.

2. Holding down the "Option" key changes the "Add" button to "Add All", letting you add all of the files and folders listed on the left side.

3. You can select a folder and add it along with all its contents to the "Items to Stuff" list.

4. You can selectively add the contents of a folder or disk using the "Add Match" button. See "Example: Creating Your Monthly and Yearly Archives," beginning on page 54, for a tutorial on using "Add Match" or see "Close-up: The Add Match Dialog," beginning on page 81, for more information.

■ You can use SpaceSaver or Magic Menu from the Finder to Stuff any file or folder into an archive. See "Chapter 3: Using StuffIt SpaceSaver" and "Chapter 7: The Tools/Utilities" for details.

■ If "Drop•Stuff" is installed and you're using System 7, you can drag the file or folder onto the drop box in the Finder. See "Example: Stuffing with Drop•Stuff," beginning on page 135, in "Chapter 7: The Tools/Utilities" for a tutorial on doing this.

Example: Selectively UnStuffing a File from an Archive

Features Explained: Open, UnStuff, "Read Me" files, Text Viewer, and Launch.

Related Topics: See "Close-up: The Archive Palette and Window," starting on page 70, and "Chapter 5: The Viewers Extensions."

Problem: You have an old project that you've archived, consisting of some graphics, word processing documents, and a "Read Me" file that describes the documents. How do you open the archive, read the pertinent "Read Me" file, and selectively UnStuff only the file you want to UnStuff?

Solution: Using StuffIt's "Text Viewer," you can view the notes to yourself that you've placed in the "Read Me" file. Then, using StuffIt Deluxe's file selection abilities, you can selectively UnStuff the file you want from the project.

1. Go to the File menu and choose "Open…"(Command-O).

A dialog will appear showing you the contents of the StuffIt Deluxe Folder.

2. Go to the "Tutorial Files" folder and open the "Sample Archive.sit" archive by double-clicking on it.

StuffIt Deluxe will open the archive and a "Preparing To View" progress dialog will immediately appear, indicating that a "Read Me" file within the archive is about to appear on your screen. When the file has finished its preparation, it will automatically present itself to view in the Text Viewer.

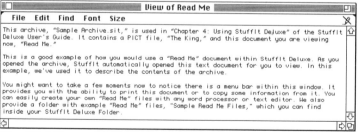

"Read Me" files are "Text" files that have been written in a word processor and saved in Text format before they're included in an archive. Saving such a file with the words "Read Me" at the beginning or end of a file name lets StuffIt automatically present it for viewing when the archive is first opened.

Note: This default automatic viewing option may be turned off. See "View 'Read Me' Files" on page 86 to learn how to turn this option on or off.

Including "Read Me" files in archives is a good practice. Instructions about the files included in the archive can be placed in "Read Me" file so that users who use the files later will know what they're for.

Note that the Text Viewer window has its own menu bar. Click each of the Viewer menus to familiarize yourself with them when you have a moment. You can also scroll through and read the text. Since you are only viewing the file, you can't edit it in this window. You can, however, select the text and copy it to the clipboard. You can also search the text or print out the contents of the "Read Me" file. See "Chapter 5: The Viewers Extensions," beginning on page 97, for more detailed information on the Text and PICT Viewers.

3. Once you're finished reading the "Read Me" file, close it by clicking the window's close box.

4. Double-click the file icon you want to UnStuff, or select the icon and drag it onto the "UnStuff" icon in the Archive Palette.

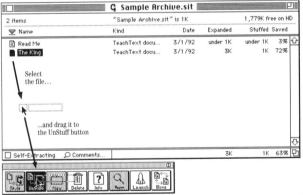

If you drag it onto the "UnStuff" icon in the Archive Palette, the "UnStuff" icon will darken when the arrow cursor is over the icon. When the icon darkens, release the mouse button.

A dialog will appear letting you rename the file or UnStuff it to another disk or folder.

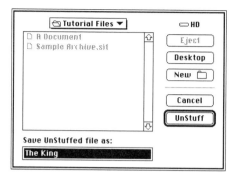

5. Give the file the name you want (if you'd like to change it) and click "UnStuff".

When you UnStuff, a progress dialog will appear indicating that the file you chose is being UnStuffed and saved to disk. You can exit StuffIt Deluxe when you're ready to use the UnStuffed file.

Alternate Methods

■ You have five ways you can UnStuff a file once an archive is open. All but the first are enabled once you've selected the file.

1. Double-click the file you want to UnStuff.

2. Click the "UnStuff" icon in the Archive Palette.

3. Drag it onto the "UnStuff" icon in the Archive Palette.

4. Choose "UnStuff…" from the Archive menu.

5. Type "Command-U".

■ When you start to open an archive by using the "Open…" command (Command-O) in the File menu, you can actually UnStuff an entire archive without really opening it. This is done by simply by selecting the archive in the "Open" dialog and clicking the "UnStuff" button within the dialog. StuffIt creates a folder with the archive's name and puts all the UnStuffed items into it.

■ You can use SpaceSaver or Magic Menu from the Finder to UnStuff any archive. See "Chapter 3: Using StuffIt SpaceSaver" and "Chapter 7: The Tools/Utilities" for details.

■ If "Drop•UnStuff" is installed and you're using System 7, you can drag the file or folder onto the Drop•UnStuff drop box in the Finder. See "Example: UnStuffing with Drop•UnStuff," beginning on page 136, in "Chapter 7: The Tools/Utilities" for a tutorial on doing this.

UnStuffing and Launching

■ The "Launch" feature within StuffIt lets you UnStuff a file and automatically launch, or open, the file if the appropriate application is on disk.

1. Select the file icon you wish to UnStuff.

2. Choose "Launch..." (Command-T) from the Archive menu, or click "Launch" in the Archive Palette.

As shown in the previous example, you can also drag an icon onto the "Launch" button in the Archive Palette.

Either way, a dialog will appear, asking you to choose a location where you want to put the file.

3. Click the "UnStuff" button.

StuffIt will UnStuff the file and launch the document if the application is available on disk. If the application is not available, a message will tell you it can't be launched.

Where To Go From Here

Now that you know some quick ways to Stuff and UnStuff files with StuffIt Deluxe, you'll want to explore all the other features of StuffIt. These features will make the process of Stuffing, archiving, backing up, and securing your files a part of your everyday work. The rest of this chapter provides examples of how to use StuffIt's more advanced features.

Section Two: Beyond the Basics

Introduction

In this section, "Beyond the Basics," we'll show you how to archive multiple files, how to do backups for files too large to fit on a floppy, how to secure files from prying eyes, and how to create archives that will UnStuff themselves even if StuffIt is not present. This section is for those who are eager to get more out of StuffIt.

Immediately following this section is "Section Three: Mastering StuffIt Deluxe," beginning on page 68, a reference for those who would like to master many of the additional features of StuffIt Deluxe. It completes the profile of the core features of the StuffIt application, and is a good preface to the following chapters on the StuffIt Extensions and the Scripting language.

Example: Creating Your Monthly and Yearly Archives

Features Explained: Stuff, Add Match, Move/Copy, Delete Item When Finished, and New Folder.

Related Topics: See "Close-up: The Add Match Dialog,"starting on page 81 in this chapter and "Chapter 8: Automating StuffIt."

Problem: You'd like to create monthly and yearly archives for backing up your files. In your monthly archives, you'd like to place only those files you've changed that month. Then, at the end of every month, you'd like to place the files and folders of your monthly archives into your yearly archive, organized by month. How do you accomplish both goals?

Solution: You create a monthly archive and, using StuffIt's "Add Match" feature, you make monthly backups of only those files that have changed that month. Then, using StuffIt's ability to create, delete, and move/copy files and folders, you're able to take files from your monthly archives and put them into your yearly archives.

There are two parts to this example, since we'll be creating two archives: a monthly archive and a yearly one. In Part One, we'll selectively add a folder with some of its contents to a monthly archive using the "Add Match" feature in the Stuff dialog. In Part Two, we'll create a yearly archive and add the files and folders from our monthly archives to it. We'll follow this two-part example with another one that shows you how to back up a large archive into segments in order to copy it to floppy disks.

Part One: Creating the Monthly Archive

Part One has you selectively add a portion of a folder to a monthly archive using the "Add Match" feature.

1. **Choose "New…" (Command-N) from the File menu and name the archive with the current month. Type "March 1992.sit", for example.**

2. **Click the "Stuff" icon in the Archive Palette or choose "Stuff" (Command-S) from the "Archive Menu".**

A dialog will appear, presenting you with the list of files and folders on your disk.

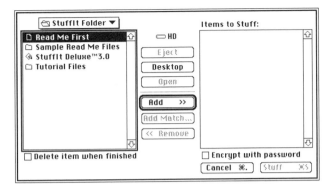

3. Click the "Tutorial Files" folder.

Clicking on any folder or disk while you're in the "Stuff" dialog activates the "Add Match…" button, letting you work on the contents of that folder or disk.

4. Click the "Add Match…" button.

The "Add Match" dialog appears, presenting you with a number of criteria you can establish to narrow the range of files that will be Stuffed within the folder or volume you're archiving. The more criteria you specify, the narrower the range of the files that are archived from that folder or volume.

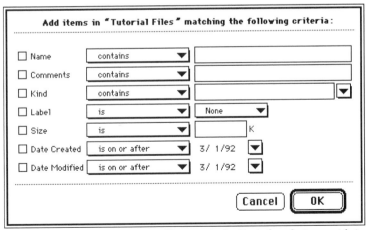

For now, we're only going to specify one set of criteria for what we put into our archive. See "Close-up: The Add Match Dialog," beginning on page 81, for a more detailed explanation of the Add Match dialog.

5. **Select the "is between" option from the "Date Modified" pop-up menu and type the range "3/1/92 to 4/1/92" so that all files that have been modified between March 1, 1992 and April 1, 1992 are added to our archive.**

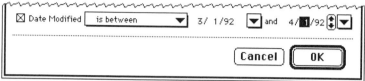

Notice how the "Date Modified" check box is automatically checked after you specify these criteria.

6. Click the "OK" button.

The folder "Tutorial Files" has been added to the list of files for archiving with a special icon to show that it will be scanned for matches. Only those files in "Tutorial Files" that have been modified between 3/1/92 and 4/1/92 will be archived.

Note: If you want to delete these files after they're Stuffed, check the "Delete Item When Finished" check box in the "Stuff" dialog before you add them to the list.

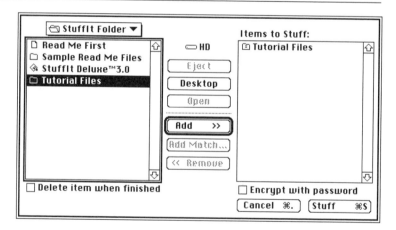

7. Click the "Stuff" button (Command-S).

A Progress Dialog will appear indicating the progress of StuffIt as it scans and Stuffs your "Tutorial Files" folder. When it's done, you'll be returned to the archive window.

You'll now notice that the folder "Tutorial Files" has been added to the archive window.

8. **Double-click the "Tutorial Files" folder in the archive to enter into it.**

   The "Tutorial Files" folder will open in the archive and display all those files in the folder which were modified between 3/1/92 and 4/1/92. Files in the original "Tutorial Files" folder that did not meet this criteria will not be Stuffed.

9. **You can move out of the "Tutorial Files" folder in the archive by choosing "March 1992.sit" in the Archive pop up menu that's part of the window's title bar.**

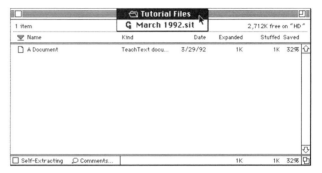

10. **You can also create new folders in the archive by clicking on the "New" folder icon in the Archive Palette or by choosing the "New Folder..." (Command-F) from the Archive Menu.**

    A new "untitled folder" will appear in the archive, with "untitled" already selected for you to rename the folder.

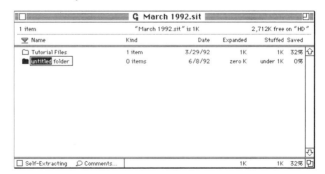

11. **Simply type the name you'd like to give to the folder and hit Return on your keyboard to save the new folder name.**

At this point you might open the folder and Stuff one or more files or folders into it. Folders within StuffIt are used like folders in the Finder with one minor exception—they're Stuffed.

Leave the "March 1992.sit" archive open as we move to Part Two of our example. If you want to take a break now, do so and return to the next part when you're ready.

Part Two: Creating the Annual Archive

In Part One of this example, you learned how to create a monthly archive and to Stuff files that changed during that month into the archive. In Part Two, you'll learn how to move the folders and files of your monthly archives into a yearly archive at the end of each month.

1. Open the "March 1992.sit" archive if it's not already open.

2. Choose "New…" (Command-N) from the File menu.

A dialog will appear letting you name the new archive.

3. Type "1992" and click the "New" button.

A "1992.sit" archive will be created and a new archive window will open. You now have two archives open simultaneously.

4. Move the "1992.sit" archive below the "March 1992.sit" archive so it will be easier to work with both archives.

If you click the zoom box in the upper right corner, StuffIt Deluxe will automatically resize the window to its narrowest vertical height. Then you can line up the windows more easily. See "Multiple Windows," beginning on page 76, for information on manipulating and positioning archive windows.

5. Select the folder "Tutorial Files" in the "March 1992.sit" archive and drag it onto the "1992.sit" window.

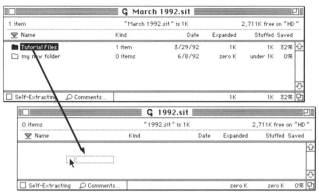

A progress dialog will appear, indicating that StuffIt Deluxe is copying the folder from the "March 1992.sit" archive to the "1992.sit" archive.

Since you've taken the "Tutorial Files" folder from the "March 1992.sit" archive, you have no way of knowing that the "Tutorial Files" folder contains those files you changed in March. We'll rename it to remind us that these are the files we archived for March.

6. Position the cursor over the "Tutorial Files" folder in the "1992.sit" archive and click.

7. Rename the entire folder to "March Archives".

8. Click elsewhere in the archive or press the "Enter" key. The folder is now renamed.

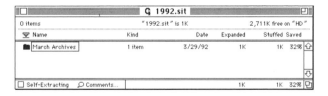

Alternate Method

■ On Macintoshes with smaller screens, it may not be practical to put two or three archives side by side. StuffIt Deluxe anticipates this and give you an alternate way to copy or move files and folders between archives. (You can also move files and folders within the same archive.) To do this, use the "Move/Copy" command.

1. Open the "1992.sit" archive, and then the "March 1992.sit" archive if they're not already open.

The second archive you open will be the active window.

2. Select the "Tutorial Files" folder in the "March 1992.sit" archive window.

3. Drag the "Tutorial Files" folder onto the "Move" icon of the Archive Palette.

A dialog will appear, displaying the contents of the current archive.

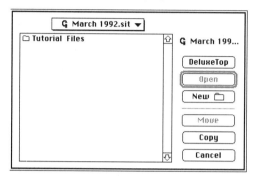

4. Click the "DeluxeTop" button in the dialog.

The list will change, showing the archives that are currently open.

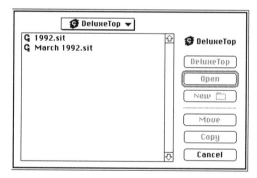

Note: The "DeluxeTop" button is the StuffIt equivalent of the "Desktop" icon in Open and Save dialogs. The "DeluxeTop" button shows you the archives that are currently open, while the "Desktop" button shows you the disks that are currently available.

5. Select the "1992.sit" archive name in the list and click the "Open" button.

You'll find yourself inside the "1992.sit" archive, and the "New Folder", "Move", and "Copy" buttons will now be active on the Palette.

6. Click the "Move" button.

StuffIt Deluxe will move "Tutorial Files" folder from the "March 1992.sit" archive to the "1992.sit" archive.

Note: Had you selected the "Copy" button here, the folder would have been copied rather than moved, and a copy of the original "Tutorial Files" folder would be retained in the "March 1992.sit" archive. This folder could be retained or deleted, as you wish.

Example: Backing Up Your Yearly Archive

Features Explained: Segment and Join.

Related Topics: None.

Problem: Now that you've created a Yearly Archive into which all your monthly archives go, you want to ensure the security of your data by making a backup of the "1992.sit" archive. After a few months, however, it's larger than your 800K diskettes. How do you back up your Yearly Archive onto multiple diskettes?

Solution: Using StuffIt's "Segmenting" feature, you split the Yearly Archive into segments for backup to several floppies. Later, using StuffIt's Join feature, you restore it to the hard drive when you need to.

Segmenting

Though we can't supply a sample archive as large as your real Yearly Archive, the following simulation of Segmenting and Joining can be easily reproduced for an actual archive.

1. Go to the "Segmenting" menu item in the Translate menu.

2. From the sub-menu that appears, choose "Segment...".

A dialog will appear.

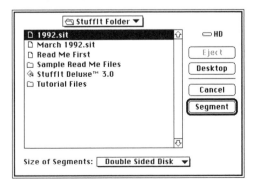

3. Select the archive that you want to segment.

4. Choose the appropriate disk size from the "Size of Segments:" pop-up menu at the bottom of the dialog or choose "Other..." if one of the preset sizes isn't appropriate.

If you choose "Other...", you'll be presented with a dialog which lets you enter the size of the segment that you want. Choosing "Maximum Possible" will tell StuffIt to use every bit of disk space available on the disks you segment onto.

5. Click the "Segment" button in the main dialog and another dialog appears so you can save the first segment.

StuffIt automatically adds a suffix for the number of the segment (e.g., ".1") after the name of the file you're segmenting. It's best to leave the name unchanged in this case; it makes it easier to join the segments later.

6. If you want to save directly to a diskette, insert an empty, formatted diskette now and the diskette name appears. Click "Save" to place the first segment on this diskette. (If you had a hard disk, you would go to the folder in which you wanted to save the first segment and click "Save".)

Note: If the diskette you insert is not already empty, you may choose to use the "Erase Floppy" button which will clear the diskette of all files. Use this with caution because you may have important files on the diskette.

After you click "Save", a progress dialog appears which shows StuffIt's progress as it segments the file. When StuffIt has completed the first segment, it ejects the first diskette and asks you to insert the second diskette. When you do, a dialog appears so you can enter a name for the second segment. As before, the default name is best, so just click "Save". StuffIt will continue this process until it has finished segmenting the file.

Alternate Method

■ When you segment a file to a hard disk, you can automatically create several segments by clicking the "Save All" button instead of the "Save" button in the Segment dialog. StuffIt will automatically divide the file into as many segments as it needs.

Joining

The "Join…" command lets you join files that you've split using the "Segment…" command. In this example, we join the same file you previously split onto several floppies.

1. Choose "Segmenting" from the Translate menu.

2. When the sub-menu appears, choose "Join…".

StuffIt prompts you to locate the first segment of the file that you want to join.

3. Insert the diskette containing the first segment.

If you segmented to a hard disk, go to the location of the segmented files.

4. Select the segment with the ".1" suffix and click Open.

A Save dialog appears, prompting you to go to the location where you want the joined file to be saved.

5. Once you've picked the location for the joined file, click "Save".

A progress dialog appears as StuffIt assembles the segments of the file. After StuffIt has assembled the first segment, it will eject the first disk and prompt you for the second segment.

6. Insert the disk with the second segment.

StuffIt continues joining the file, prompting you for more diskettes until the joining process is completed. When StuffIt has joined all the segments, it will tell you it's done.

Alternate Method

■ When you join segments that have been saved onto a hard drive, StuffIt automatically joins the segments if they've been saved in the same folder and have retained their original names. You simply select the first segment when you're joining and StuffIt automatically locates the following segments as it completes the join.

Example: Securing Files for Sending

Features Explained: Encryption Preferences, Passwords, and Change Password.

Related Topics: See "Encryption" on page 93 for setting encryption and passwords on by default.

Problem: You have some files with sensitive information that you want to send to your friend over the network or over the phone lines, but you're concerned about prying eyes. How do you protect your files?

Solution: Using StuffIt Deluxe's encryption and password system, you secure your archive by scrambling its contents with a password that you establish. Later, only people who know the password can retrieve items from the protected archive.

WARNING: If you forget an archive's password, there is no way to recover the information or to modify the secured contents of the archive. Aladdin Systems does not have a way to decrypt archives. Be sure to remember your passwords or write them down and put them in a safe place.

---

1. Choose "New…" (Command-N) from the File menu.

2. Name the new archive "Secure.sit" and click the "New" button.

A new archive window will appear.

3. Click the "Stuff" button in the Archive Palette or choose "Stuff…" (Command-S) from the Archive menu.

4. In the "Stuff" dialog, check the "Delete item when finished" check box to make sure no unprotected files are left lying around.

The "Delete item when finished" option will erase the files you Stuff, regardless if you choose to encrypt them or not.

5. Navigate to the "Tutorial Files" folder, open it, select a file, and click the "Add" button.

Since, in our last step, we told StuffIt to delete the item when it's Stuffed, StuffIt will prompt you to ask you if you're sure you want to permanently delete it.

6. Click the "Yes" button to tell StuffIt that you want the file deleted after it's Stuffed into the archive.

7. Check the "Encrypt with password" check box below the "Items to Stuff" list on the right.

Note: If you plan on encrypting items time and again, you can set an preference option to always have "Encrypt with password" checked. See "Encryption" on page 93 for information on using that preference setting.

8. Click the "Stuff" button.

A dialog will appear asking you to enter a password.

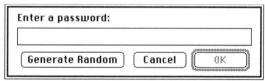

Anything that can be typed from your keyboard is acceptable in the password, including international characters. A good password is alphanumeric, easy for you (but not someone else) to remember, and long. Since passwords are case-sensitive, you can make your password more difficult to break by adding capital letters in places. If you can't think of a password, StuffIt can generate a random one for you. A random password will probably not be easy for you to remember, so use the "Generate Random" button with discretion.

Note: The minimum length of the password is three characters.

9. Enter a password in the text box and click the "OK" button.

StuffIt prompts you to re-enter your password to verify that you typed what you wanted to type.

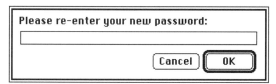

10. Enter your password a second time and click the "OK" button.

When you've entered the correct password, StuffIt will Stuff the files or folders into the archive and a "key" icon appears in the archive next to the document icons.

This indicates that the file is secured with a password. Since you're already in the archive, you can now add more files to it without having to re-enter the password. When you open the archive in future sessions, however, and attempt to add, delete, modify, or UnStuff files or folders that contain encrypted files, StuffIt will again ask you for a password.

At any time, you may choose to change the password of the archive. This is done using the "Change Password" command in the Translate menu.

1. Begin by choosing "Change Password" from the Translate menu.

2. In the dialog that appears, enter your existing password and the new password that you want the archive to have, and click the "OK" button.

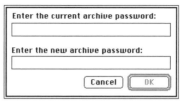

Enter the current archive password:

Enter the new archive password:

Cancel   OK

StuffIt prompts you to re-enter your password to verify that you typed what you wanted to type.

3. Enter your new password a second time and click the "OK" button.

That's it. From now on, you'll need to use the new password to work with the encrypted items in the archive.

Example: Self-Extracting Archives

Features Explained: Creating a Self-Extracting Archive and Launching a Self-Extracting Archive.

Related Topics: For a tutorial on doing this from the Finder with SpaceSaver, see "Example: Sending a Folder to a Friend," beginning on page 22, in "Chapter 3: Using StuffIt SpaceSaver" and "Make Self-Extracting Preferences," beginning on page 144, in "Chapter 7: The Tools/Utilities."

Problem: Occasionally you have to send an archive to someone who doesn't have any StuffIt product. How can he/she open a StuffIt archive without the software?

Solution: You Stuff the file using StuffIt's "Self-Extracting" feature. This creates a mini-application that can be launched from the Finder.

Creating a "Self-Extracting" archive is an easy task.

1. Choose "New..." (Command-N) from the File menu.

2. Stuff some files into the new archive.

3. Click the "Self-Extracting" check box in the lower left corner of the archive window.

A progress dialog will appear indicating that StuffIt is converting the archive to a self-extracting archive. When StuffIt is finished, the check box will be checked.

StuffIt will rename your archive, changing the ".sit" suffix to ".sea". With the ".sea" suffix, you can instantly tell that the archive is of a self-extracting type.

4. Close the archive and it will be saved on disk as a self-extracting archive.

You can now send the self-extracting archive to another person. The icon in the Finder looks like this:

Book Folder.sea

Anybody can expand the file simply by double-clicking on it. A dialog will ask them where the expanded folder should be placed and that's all they need to do.

Alternate Method

■ In the Finder, you can use SpaceSaver or Magic Menu to make self-extracting archives. See "Chapter 3: Using StuffIt SpaceSaver" and "Chapter 7: The Tools/Utilities" for details.

Section Three: Mastering StuffIt Deluxe

Introduction

Now that you've gone through the tutorials, you'll want to expand your knowledge of StuffIt Deluxe. In this section we cover basic features and procedures in StuffIt Deluxe, but we give you a close-up look at them. Be sure to read chapters 5 through 8 for more information on the extensions to StuffIt's abilities.

Close-up: The Open and Save As Dialogs

Features Explained: Open and Save As.

Related Topics: See "Example: Self-Extracting Archives," beginning on page 67, in this chapter.

Almost every Macintosh application has "Open…" and "Save As" commands in the "File" menu and StuffIt is no exception. StuffIt, however, doesn't have "Save" command. This is because StuffIt is always saving archives as you Stuff files into them. This "Close-up" delves into the options and uses for StuffIt's "Open…" and "Save As…" commands.

Open

The "Open…" (Command-O) command will bring up an Open dialog that has a "Show" pop-up menu at the bottom of the dialog.

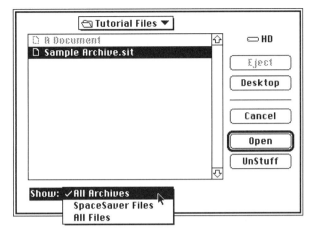

Choosing "All Archives" from the "Show" pop-up menu will have the "Open" dialog only display regular archives (.sit) and self-extracting ones (.sea). Choosing "SpaceSaver Files" will cause all files compressed with SpaceSaver to appear. Opening a SpaceSaver file will decompress it in place. This option is provided for the rare time that you will have SpaceSaver off and need to access a compressed file. The third menu choice, "All Files", will have every file on your disk appear in the dialog. Use this with extreme caution. StuffIt will always warn you if the file you're opening cannot be used.

Save As

The "Save As…" command allows you to save an open archive in another location and optionally rename it at the same time. When you choose "Save As…" from the File menu, you'll be presented with a "Save" dialog.

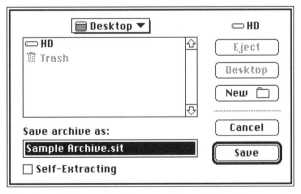

This Save dialog works like every Save dialog. You can also check the "Self-Extracting" check box and save an archive as a self-extracting archive. You can use this command to save a self-extracting archive so that you can keep both the original archive and have a self-extracting version of it.

Close-up: The Archive Palette and Window

Features Explained: The Archive Palette, Archive Window, Dragging Files Onto the Archive Palette, Retiling the Archive Palette, Stack Windows, Tile Windows, Next Window, and Last Window.

Related Topics: See the examples in "Section One: The Basics of StuffIt" and "Section Two: Beyond the Basics" both in this chapter.

The two key windows in StuffIt Deluxe are the "Archive Palette" and the "Archive Window." In this section, we take a closer look at both windows, with an eye to understanding and mastering their features.

The Archive Palette

The "Archive Palette" is a very useful tool. It's a good idea to know the full range of its capabilities as soon as you can. To get a better idea of how it works, you may want to launch StuffIt and open an archive as we proceed with our explanation.

When you launch StuffIt Deluxe, and the "Archive Palette" is turned on in the Preferences dialog, the first thing that comes on screen is the "Archive Palette," a row of buttons that "floats" above archive windows. When no archive is open, all the buttons are dimmed.

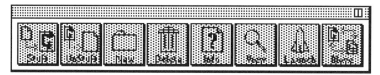

Here's how the "Archive Palette" looks when it's fully active:

Each button in the "Archive Palette" has an equivalent menu-item in the "Archive" menu (as well as command key equivalents), and just like any menu item, when the button is unavailable it's "dimmed." Here are the Archive Menu, Command Keys, and their Archive Palette equivalents.

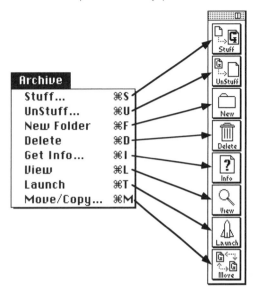

To use the Archive Palette, click an active button to initiate an operation on the file or folder that you're manipulating. You can also select an item in the "Archive Window" and drag it onto certain buttons to perform the same operation you get from selecting the item and then clicking the button. This dragging operation works for "UnStuff", "Delete", "Info", and "Move". Files, but not folders, can be dragged onto the "View" (if the file is viewable), "Launch", and "Move" buttons. The operation looks like this:

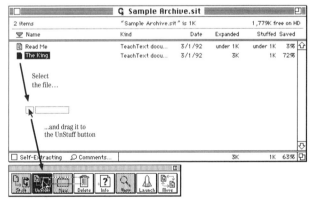

Once the cursor and outline of the selected item are over the button, it highlights. Releasing the mouse executes the command.

You can also manipulate the "Archive Palette" to make the best use of your screen real estate as you work with your archives.

Hide/Show

As shown in the "Close-up: Setting Your Preferences," beginning on page 84, you can hide or show the "Archive Palette" by checking or unchecking the "Palette" check box in the Preferences dialog available from the Edit menu.

Move

You can move the palette around on the screen by simply holding the mouse cursor down on the bar at the top of the palette and moving it to where you want it.

Retile

You can click the Retile box located in the upper right corner of the palette to toggle the palette through four tiling views:

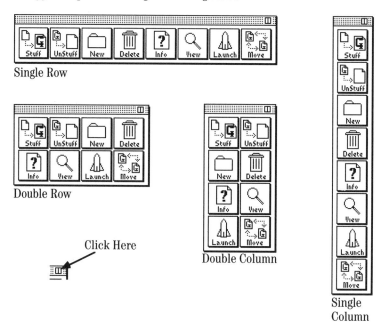

Single Row

Double Row

Click Here

Double Column

Single Column

Thus, you have four main ways to execute a command in StuffIt Deluxe:

1. You can choose the menu item from the Archive Menu.

2. You can type the Command key equivalent of the menu item.

3. When a file or folder is selected in an archive, the grayed-out icons become active and you can click the appropriate button in the Archive Palette.

4. You can drag the file or folder onto the appropriate button.

The Archive Window

When you created your first archive, you probably noticed that a new archive was created even before you put anything into it. That's because whenever you create an archive, you're immediately saving its information to disk. Let's take a look at an Archive window.

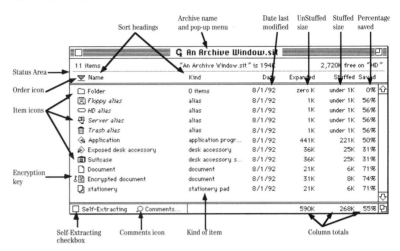

Every item Stuffed within a StuffIt archive is listed with its own kind of icon that helps you identify what kind of file it is. A key to the left of an icon indicates that an item has been encrypted.

Note too that the Archive window is like windows in most Macintosh programs (with one exception noted in the next paragraph). It has zoom and grow boxes in the upper and lower right corners, and a close box in the upper left. The name of the archive is displayed in the title bar of the archive's window. Furthermore, the archive window can be moved around by selecting its title bar with your cursor and dragging it to where you want it to be.

A fundamental difference between windows in most Macintosh programs and a StuffIt archive window appears only when you are in a folder within an archive. When you are inside a folder, the name of the folder will be shown in the title bar (in place of the archive name) and that folder name will be an active pop-up menu similar to the one in Open and Save dialogs.

Here is what you would see when inside a folder. Notice how there is a down arrow next to the folder name. This means that this is a pop-up menu.

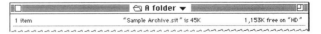

Clicking on the folder name (or the down arrow) will show the pop-up menu. Choosing any item off the pop-up menu will bring you to that folder. In this example, choosing "Sample Archive.sit" will bring you to the root level of the archive.

You can also type Command-'up arrow' to move out of a single folder. If a folder is selected, type Command-'down arrow' to enter into it.

Status Area

Also, listed above the view headers is a Status area that tells you:

• how many items are contained at the current level in the archive,

• the name of the archive and its size, and

• the amount of free space on the disk where your archive resides.

At the bottom of the archive window, two more options are available to you for modifying your archive:

View Headings

With all the relevant "View" preference settings active, your archive displays a wide range of data on your files. See "Activating Views," beginning on page 94, for adjusting the views/headings you want.

Clicking the Order icon to the left of the Name label sorts the files by the order they were entered into the archive. Clicking the Name, Kind, Label, Date, Expanded, Stuffed, or Saved heading above a list of files sorts the file list according to the view heading. Labels can be added to a file or folder from within the archive by simply selecting the item and then going to the Label menu and choosing the label you want the item in the archive to have.

Self-Extracting Check Box

One of the two options in the lower left corner of an archive window is the "Self-Extracting" check box. It is used for creating an archive that can be extracted on any Macintosh, even if there are no StuffIt products present. See "Example: Self-Extracting Archives," beginning on page 67, in "Section Two: Beyond the Basics" for the tutorial on using this check box.

Comments Icon

The other option in the lower left corner is the "Comments" icon. The "Comments" icon allows you to enter a comment into the archive. See "Comments," beginning on page 78, for details.

Selecting Items

There are many ways in which you can select one or more items in an archive window.

If you need to select multiple items, you can hold down the Command key and click the items you want in your selection. You can also use the Shift key to extend an existing selection. Once selected, you can choose a menu item or drag the selected items onto an icon to perform a command on the entire group. For example, if there are five items in an archive and the first item is selected, you can extend the selection to include items one through five by shift-clicking on the fifth item. Here we show a shift-click "July 1992 Correspondence" that extends the selection from "Mike's Folder".

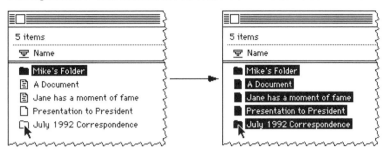

Another way of multiple items is to drag the arrow cursor around a group of items. A dashed rectangle indicates the area covered as you drag and the selected items will become highlighted. As an example, here is a selection of three items. Notice that we hold down the mouse button when we start the selection in the lower left corner.

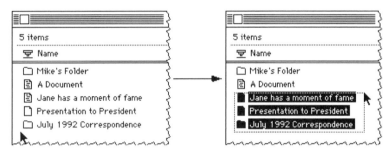

Dragging Items Within and Between Archives

As illustrated in some tutorials and in "The Archive Palette," you can drag items within archives onto icons to perform commands. You are also able to drag items into folders, to rearrange their order within an archive, or to copy items between archives.

Dragging a file or folder into an archive is simple; it's done just as you do in the Finder. You can drag one or more items into any folder icon to move it into that folder. If you wish to rearrange the order of items within an archive, you must have the Order icon view selected. Drag any file or folder that you wish to reorder to its new location. Here we drag "July 1992 Correspondence" between "A Document" and "Jane has a moment of fame". Notice the illustration on the right shows the new position of the "July 1992 Correspondence" folder.

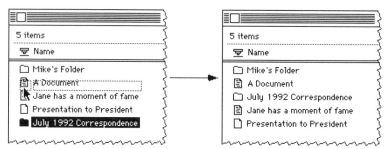

When multiple archive windows are open, you're able to drag one or more items between them. This is the same as using the "Copy" button when using the "Move/Copy" command. A duplicate of the item(s) you drag will be placed in the archive you want them in. Here we're dragging a folder into the "1992.sit" archive.

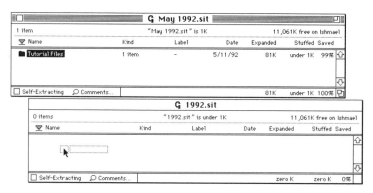

Multiple Windows

When multiple windows are open, StuffIt also gives you some extra abilities. These include the ability to move between windows from a menu and to rearrange them on the screen for easier use. You'll see these extra commands when the "Window" menu is active. See "The StuffIt Menus," beginning on page 89, for how to turn individual menus on and off.

Stack Windows

Choosing this command lets you stack windows diagonally for easy selection, stacking them first to last, the last topmost, in the order they were opened.

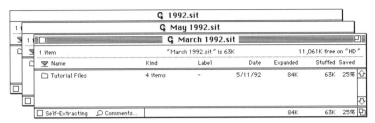

Tile Windows

Choosing this command lets you automatically tile windows to the size of your screen. StuffIt calculates the best tiling option for the number of windows you have open.

Next Window

Choosing "Next Window" (Command-]) from the Windows menu lets you descend one window down in a group of stacked windows, bringing that window to the front.

Last Window

Choosing the "Last Window" (Command-[) menu item lets you move to the last window in a group of stacked windows, bringing that window to the front.

To find out how to get more information on your archives, continue on to the next "Close-up."

Close-up: Getting/ Keeping Information on Your Archives

Features Explained: Comments, Get Info, and Print.

Related Topics: See "Example: Using On Location to Know About Files Within Archives," beginning on page 147, in "Chapter 7: The Tools/Utilities."

There are times when you want to get information about an archive. StuffIt provides you with a range of ways to do just that. Aside from enclosing "Read Me" files within an archive, you can also enter and read enclosed comments within an archive, get information on specific files and folders, and print a report that will give you full information on the files and folders in your archive.

Comments

A comment is some text that you enter into an archive that will always stay with an archive, regardless of the archive's contents. It is different from a "Read Me" file in that you can enter the text from within StuffIt. You can print the comments of an archive with the "Print…" command.

To store a comment in an archive, you need to first enter the archive.

1. Choose "Open…" (Command-O) from the File menu and open the archive you wish to attach comments to.

When the archive opens up, notice the empty "Comments…" balloon in the lower left corner of the archive window.

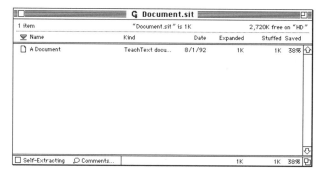

3. Click the "Comments…" balloon icon at the bottom of the window.

4. When the Comments dialog appears, type a message in the Comments field.

You can type up to 32,000 characters of information into this field, though most people type short notes. You can scroll through a long comment by selecting text and moving the mouse up and down through the editing area.

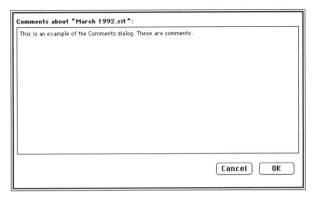

5. When you're through entering your comments, click "OK" in the Comments window.

Notice now that the "Comments…" balloon has small dots or dashes lines within it. These indicate that there are comments within the "Comments…" field.

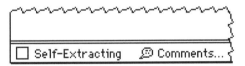

6. To read the "Comments…" field, simply click the "Comments…" balloon icon again.

Getting Information

StuffIt's "Get Info…" command in the Archive menu, or the "Info" icon in the Archive Palette gives you detailed information about the items in an archive.

1. Open an archive and select a file in the archive.

2. Choose "Get Info…" (Command-I) from the Archive menu or click the "Info" icon in the Archive Palette.

A window will appear, displaying information about the file enclosed within the archive.

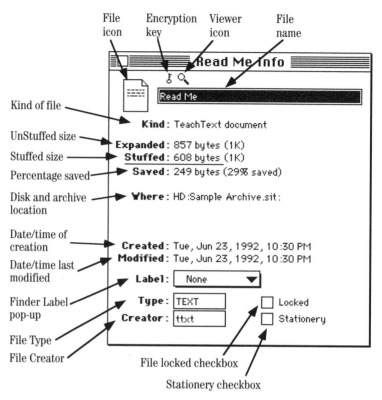

A great deal of information about the file in your archive is shown in the "Get Info" box. Additionally, the "Get Info" box lets you change the file's name in the selection rectangle, or its Label (or Color under System 6) in the pop-up menu. Checking the "Stationery" check box changes the file to a "stationery pad" and the "Kind of file" field and "Document icon" will change accordingly. Checking the "Locked" check box on an unlocked file will protect the file from deletion or alteration. If the file is already encrypted (indicated by the password key in the upper left corner of the "Get Info" box), you'll be prompted for a password before you can lock the file. If you don't know the password, you won't be able to check the "Locked" check box.

Note: If you perform a "Get Info" on a folder, you'll see a similar window. A folder Info window is the same as a file Info window except there is no Type, Creator, Locked, or Stationery item.

---

3. When you're done looking at the information about your file, click the close box in the upper left corner to close the "Get Info" window.

Print

You can print a listing of an archives contents using the "Print…" command in the File menu.

1. Choose "Print…" (Command-P) from the File menu and the standard Print dialog appears with two radio buttons added at the bottom.

• Print Report of: Entire Archive. This prints all levels and their contents.

• Print Report of: Current Level Only. This prints only the contents of the folder level that you're viewing when you choose "Print…".

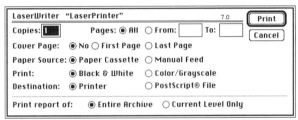

In the printed report, a header gives you the name of the file and the level from which the report has been generated. This is followed by any comments stored in the Comments balloon.

The body of the report is similar to any Finder printout of a folder and mirrors the image of your archive that you have on the screen, with its icons, column titles, sizes of files, and the like. When you choose "Entire Archive", all folders are shown "open" with their contents indented in outline format below the folder icon.

Close-up: The Add Match Dialog

Feature Explained: Add Match.

Related Topic: See "Example: Creating Your Monthly and Yearly Archives," beginning on page 54, for another example using "Add Match."

The "Add Match" dialog is a powerful tool for narrowing the criteria by which files are added to archives. With "Add Match," you can include or exclude just about any kind of file in a given folder during your archival process, using the either/or options in the various check boxes and pop-up menus.

1. Open an archive to use with this example.

2. Click the "Stuff" icon in the Archive Palette or choose "Stuff…" (Command-S) from the Archive menu.

A dialog will appear letting you select the file or folder you'd like to Stuff.

3. Select a folder in the "Stuff" dialog.

Once a folder is selected, the "Add Match" button in the "Stuff" dialog becomes available.

4. Click the "Add Match" button.

The "Add Match" dialog will open. Keep it open for the duration of this explanation.

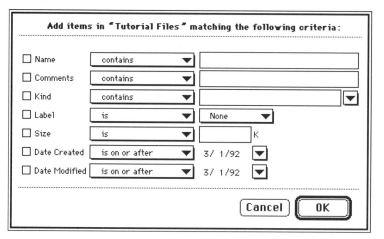

Name

Checking the "Name" check box lets you choose files you'd like to Stuff by Name. The pop-up menu lets you choose whether "Add Match" will add to the archive any file that contains or does not contain; is or is not; begins with or does not begin with; ends with or does not end with, the name you type.

Comments

Checking the "Comments" check box lets you choose files you'd like to Stuff by the comments they have in the Comments field in the Finder. The pop-up menu is identical to that for the "Name" criteria.

Kind

Checking the "Kind" check box lets you archive those files which are of a certain application Kind. Most of the pop-up options (except the last two) are identical to the Comments pop-up menu, and when they're selected, the pop-up menu on the right gives you a generic listing for Stuffing files according to whether they're an alias, application, document, extension, stationery, or suitcase.

When you select a file that is or is not of a certain type/creator, however, this activates two linked pop-up menus to the right of the Kind menu for picking the type or creator that you want.

Kind…is Type/Creator

The "type" menu appears with a list of the more popular document types (the left menu shown here) and the "creator" menu (on the right) has a list of popular applications.

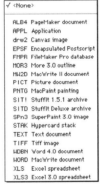

Label

Checking the "Label" check box lets you archive an item which is or is not labeled in a specific way. To choose files labeled in a certain way, you choose the linked pop-up menu to the right of the Label menu. The labels are those which display in the Macintosh Finder "Label" menu.

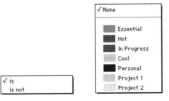

Note: Under System 6, labels will be colors only. System 6 doesn't support labels as System 7 does.

Size

Checking the "Size" check box selects a file in the folder that is or is not; is less than or greater than; is between or not between, the size you enter in the size field immediately to the right of the Size pop-up menu.

Date Created

Checking the "Date Created" check box selects a file in the folder that has been created on, after, or before; is or is not; is between or not between, the date(s) chosen in the pop-up menu(s) to the right of the Date Created menu. When you select a range option (e.g. between), a second date pop-up menu identical to the menu below appears letting you set the limits for the range.

Note that when you select the month, day, or year of the date, you can type a new number at that location, or you can use the up/down arrows to scroll through the number list. Once a day, month, or year is selected, as the number "3" is here, you can tab these three fields.

Date Modified

Checking this check box selects a file in the folder that has been modified according to the criteria in the pop-up menus for Date Modified. These menus are functionally identical to the Date Created menus, except that they specify ranges for the files' modification date, not the date of their creation.

Close-up: Setting Your Preferences

Features Explained: Preferences, Stuff Originals Instead of Aliases, Don't Stuff Already Compressed Files, Verify Writes, Convert 1.5.1 Archive on Open, Convert 1.5.1 Archive, View "Read Me" Files on Open, and Detect viruses with virus checker.

Related Topics: See "Close-up: The Archive Palette and Window," "Example: Securing Files for Sending," and "Chapter 5: The Viewers Extensions."

StuffIt has a broad range of features, many of which can be set as default preferences. We'll cover most of the settings in this section.

If you plan to read through this whole section in one sitting, leave the "Preferences…" dialog open until you're done.

1. Choose "Preferences…" from the Edit menu.

The Preferences dialog appears for you to choose your settings.

2. Set the preferences that you want to work with and click "OK" when you want to save them.

Note: StuffIt saves all your preferences in a "StuffIt Deluxe Preferences" document that's stored in the Preferences Folder within the System Folder.

The rest of this section discusses the Preferences in detail.

General Preferences

The "General" section of the Preferences dialog lets you set seven miscellaneous features within StuffIt Deluxe.

Stuff Originals Instead of Aliases

When this check box is checked and an alias is selected to be added to an archive, the original file is Stuffed instead of the alias. This option is for users of System 7 only because System 6 doesn't support aliases. StuffIt ships with the "Stuff originals instead of aliases" check box checked.

Don't Stuff Files That Are Already Compressed

When this check box is checked, files that have already been compressed (such as certain PostScript fonts, StuffIt files, and files compressed with other programs) will not be re-Stuffed. StuffIt ships with the "Don't Stuff files that are already compressed" check box checked. Just as would be expected, any time a file compressed with SpaceSaver is Stuffed into an archive, it will be transparently decompressed as it is being Stuffed into an archive. SpaceSaver treats StuffIt no differently from any other application—when a file is being opened for use, it is immediately decompressed.

Verify Writes

When the "Verify writes" preference is checked, a verification procedure is run on files as they're being Stuffed. StuffIt will read back a file that was just Stuffed into an archive and compare it to the original. This gives you extra safety when Stuffing files into archives. StuffIt ships with the "Verify Writes" check box not checked since a slight delay is created during a verification.

SpaceSaver has a similar option for when it's working. See "Verify Writes" on page 34 of "Chapter 3: Using StuffIt SpaceSaver" for setting a similar SpaceSaver preference.

Note: The Macintosh normally verifies files as they are being read or written on disk. This option is necessary only if you want an added level of protection.

Convert 1.5.1 Archives to 3.0 on Open

When this preference is checked, StuffIt automatically converts any archives created with earlier versions of StuffIt as it opens them. Converting an archive to 3.0 format does not improve the compression of the Stuffed files, but changes the file to a format where you can navigate among folders. The older 1.5.1 format would not let you move among folders and required you to work at the root level only.

StuffIt Deluxe is shipped with "Convert 1.5.1 Archives to 3.0 on Open" not checked. Checking this check box specifies that when a 1.5.1 archive is opened, it should be converted. StuffIt Deluxe also provides a command for converting individual archives into the 3.0 format. It is "Convert 1.5.1 Archive", found on the Translate menu. Regardless if you use the explicit menu command or the preferences setting, once you've converted files to the 3.0 format, you can't reconvert them to the old 1.5.1 file structure.

To achieve the better compression of this version of StuffIt Deluxe, you can use our batch conversion software. See the section "StuffIt Converter," beginning on page 145, in "Chapter 7: The Tools/Utilities" for instructions on doing this.

View "Read Me" Files on Open

When the "View 'Read Me' Files on Open" check box is checked, StuffIt uses an appropriate viewer to open a "Read Me" file in an archive. The phrase "Read Me" must appear at the beginning or end of the document name. This feature will also view files whose name begins with "About" or ends with "Doc" or "Docs". A "Read Me" file must be in the top level of the archive. StuffIt is shipped with "View 'Read Me' Files on Open" checked. This feature will not work on password-secured "Read Me" files. If you don't want StuffIt to automatically open "Read Me" files, uncheck this option. See "Chapter 5: The Viewers Extensions" for details on using viewers.

Detect Viruses With…

This option is one of StuffIt's "Apple events" features and will only work with System 7 since System 6 doesn't support Apple events. In order to use this feature, you must have virus detection software that support Apple events. Contact the vendor of your virus detection software to see if the version you have supports Apple events. See the section "Apple events" in "Chapter 8: Automating StuffIt" for a further explanation of Apple events.

When this check box is checked and you're UnStuffing a file, StuffIt will open the specified virus software and have it check the UnStuffed file for viruses. If a file is corrupted with a virus, that product will tell you the file is not to be used. StuffIt ships with the "Virus Checking" option off.

To establish a link between StuffIt Deluxe and an Apple event-aware virus product, click the "Select…" button. An "Open" dialog will appear asking you to locate the anti-virus software.

New Folder Suffix

The "New Folder Suffix:" option lets you pre-select a suffix for a folder when you click the Folder icon in the Archive palette, or select New Folder from the Archive menu. StuffIt is shipped with " folder" chosen for you. You can rename the suffix anything you'd like. Remove the suffix if you want to create new folder names without a predefined suffix.

Activating the StuffIt Palette and Menus

Features Explained: The StuffIt Menus and the Archive Palette.

Related Topics: See"Close-up: The Archive Palette and Window," beginning on page 70, in this chapter and in "Chapter 6: Network/Communication Extensions," see "Section One: Using StuffIt to Translate Files." Also, in "Chapter 8: Automating StuffIt," see "Section One: Scripting Within StuffIt."

StuffIt has a user-definable structure that lets both beginners and experts feel comfortable with it. By setting your "Palette" and "Menu" preferences, you're able to turn on or off the Palette or various StuffIt Menus, depending upon your preferred way of working.

When you installed StuffIt Deluxe, the Archive Palette was turned on by default, as you already saw when you loaded StuffIt for the first time.

We also pre-selected six active menus for you:

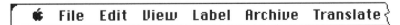

You can change these settings to customize the Palette and menu bar.

The Archive Palette

When you installed StuffIt Deluxe, we turned on the Archive Palette by default since many users find the Palette the easiest way to use StuffIt. This Palette may be turned off and you can execute all your commands from the menus or keyboard. If you turn off the Palette, however, you must have the Archive menu turned on in order to access the main features of StuffIt. See the "The StuffIt Menus" on page 89 for details.

Colorizing Palette Buttons

Additionally, if you're using a color monitor, you can colorize the buttons in the Archive Palette to your liking.

1. If it's not already selected, click the "Palette" check box to turn on the Palette.

2. Click one of the buttons to open the Color Picker.

The Apple Color Picker will appear, letting you select a color for the button in the Archive Palette.

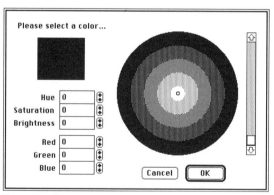

You can adjust the color wheel with the scroll bar on the right or by entering values into the edit boxes.

Note: For more information on the Color Picker, see your Macintosh Owner's Guide.

---

3. Select a color for the button and clicking "OK".

Copying Button Colors

You can also copy a color from one button to another without going through the color picker. To copy a color,

1. **Hold down the Option key on your keyboard, and the arrow cursor becomes a dropper.**

2. **Move the empty dropper over a button and click.**

The dropper picks up the color from the button.

3. **Continue holding down the Option key to have the dropper "hold" the color.**

4. **Move the dropper over the button you want the color copied to and click that icon.**

This makes the dropper "release" the color it was holding onto the current button and completes the color transfer.

The StuffIt Menus

```
┌ Menus: ─────────────────────────────────────────────────┐
│ ┌──────────────────────────────────────────────────────┐ │
│ │ ⬢ File Edit  View  Label  Archive  Translate         │ │
│ └──────────────────────────────────────────────────────┘ │
│   ☒ View              ☒ Archive          ☐ Script        │
│   ☒ Label             ☒ Translate        ☐ Window        │
└──────────────────────────────────────────────────────────┘
```

Default Settings

```
┌ Menus: ─────────────────────────────────────────────────────┐
│ ┌──────────────────────────────────────────────────────────┐ │
│ │ ⬢ File Edit  View  Label  Archive  Translate  Script  Window │ │
│ └──────────────────────────────────────────────────────────┘ │
│   ☒ View              ☒ Archive          ☒ Script           │
│   ☒ Label             ☒ Translate        ☒ Window           │
└──────────────────────────────────────────────────────────────┘
```

All Menus Active

The "Menus" section of the Preferences dialog lets you turn most of the menus within StuffIt Deluxe on or off. You'll notice first that the "File" and "Edit" are dimmed and not available for checking. These menus must always be active in any Macintosh application.

Two menus, "View" and "Label", look and work the same as the "View" and "Label" menus found at the Finder. The remaining four menus are specific to StuffIt Deluxe. Turning them on activates the full range of StuffIt's capabilities. StuffIt gives you the option of turning them on and off because some users may wish to expand or simplify StuffIt's interface in their daily work. For example, a user may not require the use of StuffIt's translation (the "Translate" menu) or scripting (the "Script" menu) capabilities and may want to turn them off.

When using this preference for the first time, you'll notice that the "View", "Label", "Archive", and "Translate" menus will be available when you install StuffIt the first time. In the examples below, we're going to turn them all on and describe the menus individually.

The View Menu

The View menu is the same as found in the Finder. It helps you sort your files. The View menu lets you do the same thing for files within archives, but StuffIt adds "Order", "View by Expanded (Size)", "View by Stuffed (Size)", and "View by (Percentage) Saved" to help sort by these criteria within StuffIt.

The Label Menu

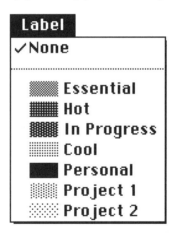

The Label menu is the same as found in the Finder. Most people use it to assist in prioritizing files and folders. The SpaceSaver portion of this package allows you to use the Label menu from the Finder to specify files to be compressed. See "Chapter 3: Using StuffIt SpaceSaver" for more information on this feature.

Using the Label menu lets you assign labels to files or folders within archives. In System 6, these labels are color names.

Note: System 7 users can change the color and/or the name of each label. This is done with the Labels control panel. See the Macintosh Owners Manual for instructions.

Labels may be assigned to files before or after they are Stuffed into archives. Files may later be sorted by Label, using the "View" menu described above. Files sorted by Labels are prioritized from the top down. In this example, files labeled with "Essential" will be sorted by View at the top of a list of files within an archive and files labeled with "Project 2" will be sorted second to the bottom. Files that do not have labels ("None") will be sorted at the bottom when the Label View is selected.

The Archive Menu

Archive	
Stuff...	⌘S
UnStuff...	⌘U
New Folder	⌘F
Delete	⌘D
Get Info...	⌘I
View	⌘L
Launch	⌘T
Move/Copy...	⌘M

Activating the "Archive" menu lets you execute the main StuffIt commands from the menu. Deactivating the "Archive" menu removes the menu from use. You must either have the "Archive" menu or the "Archive Palette" active if you want to use the main features of StuffIt Deluxe and their Command key equivalents. The "Archive" menu and the "Archive Palette" may be active at the same time.

The Translate Menu

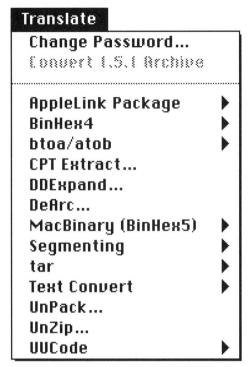

Translate

Change Password...
Convert 1.5.1 Archive
- - - - - - - - - - - -
AppleLink Package   ▶
BinHex4   ▶
btoa/atob   ▶
CPT Extract...
DDExpand...
DeArc...
MacBinary (BinHex5) ▶
Segmenting   ▶
tar   ▶
Text Convert   ▶
UnPack...
UnZip...
UUCode   ▶

Activating the "Translate" menu lets you access the file translation extensions that come with the StuffIt application. Depending upon which translators you've installed, their commands will be listed in this menu. With the "Translate" menu, you have a range of functions available to you.

Change Password

With the "Change Password..." command, you can change the password of your archive. In this chapter, see "Example: Securing Files for Sending," beginning on page 64, for a tutorial on this.

Convert 1.5.1 Archive

With the "Convert 1.5.1 Archive" command, you can convert archives from earlier StuffIt formats to optimize their use with the current version of StuffIt Deluxe. Converting an archive to 3.0 format does not improve the compression of the Stuffed files, but changes the file to a format where you can navigate among folders. The older 1.5.1 format would not let you move among folders and required you to work at the root level only.

Segmenting

From the "Segmenting" hierarchical menu, you can "Segment..." or "Join..." large StuffIt archives that you've created. For a tutorial on Segmenting, see "Example: Backing Up Your Yearly Archive," beginning on page 61, in this chapter.

Translators

You can translate files from other file formats, other computers, and other compression programs. In "Chapter 6: Network/Communication Extensions," see "Section One: Using StuffIt to Translate Files" for a detailed explanation of using translators.

The Script Menu

Activating the "Script" menu lets you record scripts, execute them, and add scripts to the "Script" menu using the "Edit Script..." command (Command-E). See "Section One: Scripting Within StuffIt," beginning on page 151, in "Chapter 8: Automating StuffIt" for a detailed explanation of this menu.

The Window Menu

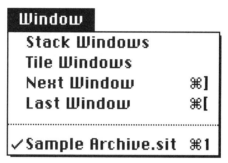

Activating the "Window" menu lets you switch between multiple archives, viewer or "info" windows that are open at the same time. Once you're used to moving files between archives, having the Windows menu active is a handy tool. See "Multiple Windows" starting on page 76 in this chapter for more on the Windows menu.

The Default Stuffing Settings

Two StuffIt settings for determining how files are Stuffed are available in the "Default Stuffing Settings" section of the Preferences dialog.

Default Stuffing Settings:
☒ Compression
☐ Encryption

Compression

Checking this check box automatically compresses files when they're Stuffed. Turning this option off lets you Stuff files without compressing them. You might want to do this if you want files to be encrypted without being compressed. Of course, StuffIt ships with the "Compression" check box checked.

Encryption

Checking this check box automatically sets files for encryption when Stuffing. When you turn this preference on, the "Encrypt With Password" option in the Stuff dialog will always be checked so you'll automatically be prompted for a password when Stuffing a file. StuffIt ships with the "Encryption" check box off.

Activating Views

```
┌ Views: ──────────────────────────────────┐
│ ⊠ Show kind                               │
│ ☐ Show label        Show sizes in:        │
│ ⊠ Show date          ⊙ kilobytes (K)      │
│ ⊠ Show expanded      ○ bytes              │
│ ⊠ Show stuffed                            │
│ ⊠ Show saved                              │
│ · · · · · · · · · · · · · · · · · · · · · │
│ ⊠ Show archive info in header             │
│ ⊠ Show directory popup without ⌘ key      │
└───────────────────────────────────────────┘
```

When you activate the "Views" titles for the Archive Window, you provide yourself with a good deal of information about your archive.

Show Kind

Checking this check box displays the kind of file it is that you've archived (i.e., TeachText, MacWrite, MacDraw, etc.).

Show Label

Checking this check box displays any Finder Label you've assigned to the file (i.e., Hot, Cool, etc.).

Show Date

Checking this check box displays, in the archive, the date the file was last modified by an application.

Show Expanded

Checking this check box displays the Expanded (UnStuffed) size of the file.

Show Stuffed

Checking this check box displays the Stuffed size of the file in the archive.

Show Saved

Checking this check box displays the percentage of disk space you've saved by archiving the file.

Show Archive Info In Header

Checking this check box displays three things in the header area: the number of items in the archive, the archive's size, and the available space on the disk where the archive resides.

Show Directory Pop-up Without Command Key

Checking this check box automatically displays a pop-up menu arrow to the right of the archive's directory name whenever you're within a folder within an archive. Unchecking it means that you must first press the Command key to display the directory pop-up in an archive.

Show Sizes In

Clicking the first radio button shows archived file sizes in kilobytes format (e.g., 2K); clicking the second radio button shows them in bytes format (e.g., 2000). In kilobytes format, file sizes are rounded correctly to the nearest kilobyte.

Where To Go From Here

Now that you've gone through StuffIt's main features, you're going to want to explore the other features of StuffIt Deluxe by reading any of the following chapters. If you're interested in learning about something specific, turn to the Table of Contents at the beginning of this User's Guide and look for your topic of interest.

Chapter 5:
The Viewers Extensions

Introduction

StuffIt Deluxe comes with Text and PICT Viewers which allow you to examine Text and PICT documents before you UnStuff them. StuffIt indicates that a viewer is available for a particular document by activating the View button in the Archive Palette when the document is selected. Choosing "View" from the Archive menu, clicking the View button, or dragging the document onto it, opens the document for viewing.

Example: Sending a Print Job to a Service Bureau

Features Explained: Text Viewer, PICT Viewer, and "Read Me" documents.

Related Topics: See "Example: Selectively UnStuffing a File from an Archive" and the "View "Read Me" Files on Open" preferences setting, both in "Chapter 4: Using StuffIt Deluxe."

Problem: You're sending graphic documents in a StuffIt archive to your local service bureau for color processing. You have specific instructions on which files should be given priority, on scaling details, on their placement in your publication, and so on. How do you enclose instructions with the archive and make sure the operator reads them before proceeding?

Solution: You enclose a text "Read Me" file along with the PICT documents in which you give instructions to the operator. When the operator opens the archive, he/she reads the "Read Me" file with StuffIt's Text Viewer. (If the recipient has the automatic "View 'Read Me' files on open" option checked in his/her own StuffIt Preferences, the "Read Me" file automatically opens in the Text Viewer when the operator opens the archive.) Then, using StuffIt's PICT Viewer, the operator scans the archive to preview the files before processing them.

First, you need to prepare a text file for your instructions to the bureau. (We've created a sample "Read Me" file for this example and have already

Stuffed it into a "Sample Archive" for you. You can use this file if you'd like to skip items 1 through 3 in this example.)

1. Using your favorite word processor, create a file called "Read Me". In it, write your instructions for the bureau, making sure you save them in text format.

All word processors allow you to save files in text format. This is usually done in the Save dialog. Consult the user's guide for your word processor for details on how to do this.

2. Create an archive called "Sample Archive.sit" and Stuff the "Read Me" file into it.

"Read Me" files must be in the root directory of the archive to automatically be read by the Text Viewer. (Do not Stuff them within a folder.) When a "Read Me" text document is Stuffed, StuffIt displays small lines in the file's icon to show that it's a text file.

3. Stuff the graphic documents into the archive, quit StuffIt Deluxe and send the archive to the service bureau.

4. When the bureau receives the archive and opens it (which you can do now for purposes of this example), instruct them to read the "Read Me" file before proceeding.

If they're using StuffIt Deluxe and they've maintained their default StuffIt Preference setting for "View 'Read Me' files on Open", a progress dialog will appear when they open the archiving telling them that StuffIt is automatically preparing the "Read Me" file for viewing. When the file is ready for viewing, it will open in the Text Viewer window.

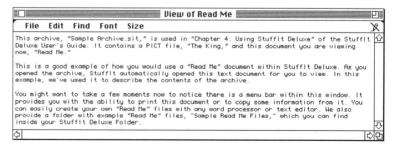

The Text Viewer window presents the text document you prepared, displayed in a window with its own menu bar. You can copy text from it and paste it into a word processing document or change the font or size of the characters while viewing it (though changes apply to the whole document, not just selected text). Since it's a read-only window, however, you can't make any changes to the document here. If you UnStuff the file, you may modify it further in your word processor.

Note: For "Read Me" files to automatically open, the phrase "Read Me" must appear at the beginning or end of the document name. This feature will also view files whose name begins with "About" or ends with "Doc" or "Docs". A "Read Me" file must be in the top level of the archive. This will not work on password-secured "Read Me" files. This feature requires that the preference for automatically viewing "Read Me" files is on. For more information on this preference, see the heading "View 'Read Me' files on Open" on page 86 in "Chapter 4: Using StuffIt Deluxe."

The PICT files in the archive can be previewed by the PICT Viewer in a similar way.

1. Close the Text Viewer.

2. Select the PICT file you wish to view and either click on the "View" icon in the Archive palette or drag the file onto it.

A progress dialog will appear, telling you that the PICT file is being prepared for viewing. In a few seconds, the PICT Viewer will present the file on the screen.

The PICT Viewer is similar to the Text Viewer, with its own menu bar You can also select portions of the image and Copy it (using the menu bar within the PICT Viewer window) into the Clipboard and paste it elsewhere.

Note: A PICT document can also be a "Read Me" if it meets the "Read Me" naming criteria.

For more information on the Text and PICT Viewers, and the Viewer menus, read on.

Text Viewer: Menus Defined

Text Viewer File menu

The File menu contains the commands for saving and printing the contents of the viewer window.

File
About Text Viewer...
Save As...   ⌘S
Page Setup...
Print...   ⌘P
Close   ⌘W

About Text Viewer...

The "About Text Viewer..." command displays a dialog with the Text Viewer's version and copyright information.

Save As...

The "Save As..." command (Command-S) allows you to save a copy of the file outside the archive. When you choose "Save As...", a standard Save dialog appears. You can select the location where you want to save the file and rename it if you like.

Page Setup...

The "Page Setup..." command lets you choose your printing options. When you choose "Page Setup...", the standard Page Setup dialog appears.

Print...

The "Print..." command (Command-P) allows you to print the contents of the viewer window. When you choose "Print...", a print dialog appears. The selected printer determines which print dialog you will see.

Close

The "Close" command (Command-W) closes the viewer window.

Text Viewer Edit Menu

The Edit menu contains the standard editing commands. Since this is a read-only document, you can't edit the text, so the "Undo", "Cut", and "Paste" commands are not available. You can select any or all of the text for copying.

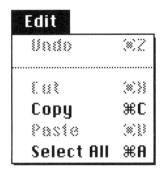

Copy

The "Copy" command (Command-C) lets you copy information from the viewer window and paste it into any text editor or word processor for editing.

Select All

The "Select All" command (Command-A) lets you select all of the text in the viewer window.

Text Viewer Find Menu

The Find menu lets you search for a text string in the viewer window.

Find...

The "Find..." command (Command-F) lets you enter some text to search for. When you choose "Find...", a "Find what:" dialog appears so you can enter a text string.

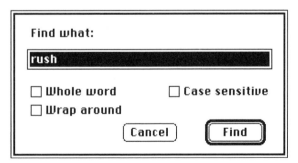

Enter the word or words you are searching for in the text box. You can also make your search more specific by checking one or all of the check boxes in the dialog.

Whole Word	Checking the "Whole word" check box ensures that only whole instances of the word will be found. For example, checking "Whole Word" causes the viewer to locate "rush" and ignore "rushing", if your search text were "rush".
Case Sensitive	Checking the "Case Sensitive" check box makes the viewer discriminate between upper and lowercase as it searches. For example, checking "Case Sensitive" causes the viewer to locate "rush" and ignore "Rush", if your search text were "rush".
Wrap Around	Checking the "Wrap Around" check box ensures a complete search. This means that a search begun in the middle of a document will wrap back to the beginning and continue through the document before it finishes scanning.
Find Next	The "Find Next" command (Command-G) causes the viewer to search for the next occurrence of the current search string.

Text Viewer Font Menu

The Font menu lets you change the font that the text is displayed in for the document you're viewing. Selecting a different font from the menu changes the view of all of the text in the window. This change is not saved when you close the viewer and exit the file, but only when you choose "Save As…" in the viewer's File menu and save a copy of the document outside the archive.

```
┌─────────────┐
│ Font        │
├─────────────┤
│  Chicago    │
│  Courier    │
│  Geneva     │
│  Helvetica  │
│ ✓Monaco     │
│  New York   │
│  Palatino   │
│  Symbol     │
│  Times      │
└─────────────┘
```

Text Viewer Size Menu

The Size menu lets you change the size of the type for the entire window.

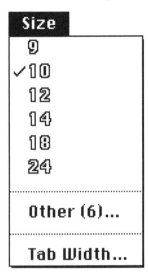

9, 10, 12, 14, 18, 24

These point sizes are some of the more popular sizes used. If the size you wish to view is not here, use the "Other..." menu choice.

Other (6)...

Choosing this command brings up a dialog to select a type size that is not available on the menu.

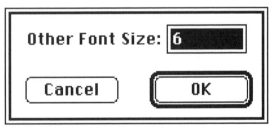

To change the type size for viewing or printing, type in the size that you want and click "OK".

Tab Width...

Choosing "Tab Width..." brings up a dialog that will let you change the number of spaces per tab.

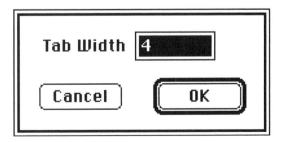

To change a tab width for viewing or printing, type in the number of spaces for the tab width you want and click "OK".

PICT Viewer:　Menus Defined

PICT Viewer File Menu

The File menu contains the commands for saving and printing the contents of the viewer window.

```
┌─────────────────────────────────┐
│ File                            │
├─────────────────────────────────┤
│   About PICT Viewer...          │
│ ································ │
│   Save As...              ⌘S   │
│ ································ │
│   Page Setup...                 │
│   Print...                      │
│ ································ │
│   Close                   ⌘W   │
└─────────────────────────────────┘
```

About PICT Viewer...

The "About PICT Viewer..." command displays a dialog with the PICT Viewer's version and copyright information.

Save As...

The "Save As..." command (Command-S) allows you to save a copy of the file outside the archive. When you choose "Save As...", a Save dialog appears. You can select the folder where you want to save the file and rename it.

Page Setup...

The "Page Setup..." command lets you choose your printing options. When you choose "Page Setup...", the standard Page Setup dialog appears.

Print...

The "Print..." command (Command-P) allows you to print the contents of the PICT Viewer window. When you choose "Print..." from the viewer's File menu, a print dialog appears.

Close

The "Close" command (Command-W) closes the viewer window.

PICT Viewer Edit Menu

The Edit Menu in the PICT Viewer window lets you select and copy the document to the Clipboard.

```
┌─────────────────────┐
│ Edit                │
├─────────────────────┤
│  Undo          ⌘Z   │
│ ................... │
│  Cut           ⌘X   │
│  Copy          ⌘C   │
│  Paste         ⌘V   │
│  Select All    ⌘A   │
└─────────────────────┘
```

Select All

The "Select All" command (Command-A) creates a selection marquee around the outer borders of the document.

Copy

The "Copy" command (Command-C) places the image of a selected document into the Clipboard. This image can be pasted into the Scrapbook or into any graphics program that supports PICT.

Where To Go From Here

This concludes our discussion of the Text and PICT Viewers. You can continue to explore the other features of StuffIt Deluxe by starting in any one of the following chapters or by take a quick look at the Table of Contents for help in finding a topic you're interested in learning about.

Chapter 6: Network/ Communication Extensions

Introduction

In the modern world, no Macintosh is an island. Macintoshes are connected to each other over local area networks (LANs), where they communicate using file servers and electronic mail. Macintoshes can also communicate to MS-DOS PCs, Digital VAXen, and Unix machines through direct connections or telecommunication programs.

StuffIt is especially designed to help you manage these foreign files.

• Using features available in the Translate menu, StuffIt can translate files created by other archiving programs and other computers.

• Using the Magic Menu mailing options, you can Stuff and send archives over a network using E-mail programs such as CE Software's QuickMail and Microsoft Mail.

• Stuffing and UnStuffing can be integrated into telecommunications programs such as MicroPhone II and White Knight.

Section One: Using StuffIt to Translate Files

Example: The Service Bureau

Features Explained: Foreign Archive Formats: AppleLink, CPT Extract, UnZip, DeArc, UnPack, tar; Different Data Formats: BinHex, Binary to ASCII, DD Expand, MacBinary, UUCode, and Text Convert.

Related Topics: See the section "The Translate Menu," on page 92, in "Chapter 4: Using StuffIt Deluxe," "Chapter 7: The Tools/Utilities," and "Chapter 8: Automating StuffIt."

Problem: You operate a service bureau that handles a wide variety of computerized printing services for both corporate business and desktop publishing accounts. Your clients use a wide range of programs and computers, and are accustomed to mailing files from all over the country via MCI, Compuserve, or the Internet. You not only have to receive a variety of archival and data formats from these clients, you need to be able to send them back after you've worked on them, saving them in the right format so they will transfer properly over the various networks.

Solution: Using StuffIt's Translators, you're able to translate files from other archival programs and other computers. Since you do this on a regular basis, you automate your E-mail and telecommunication links so that you don't have to reconstruct them every time you use them.

If the Translate menu is turned off, you need to turn it on before you can translate foreign files into StuffIt format. Following are the steps for doing this. (See "The StuffIt Menus," beginning on page 89, in "Chapter 4: Using StuffIt Deluxe" for details.)

1. Choose "Preferences..." from StuffIt's Edit menu.

A dialog will appear with menu choices available to you in the "Menus" section of the dialog.

2. Check the "Translate" check box to turn on the menu.

3. Click "OK".

The Translate menu will now be active and you can proceed with the explanations below.

```
┌─────────────────────────┐
│ Translate               │
├─────────────────────────┤
│ Change Password...      │
│ Convert 1.5.1 Archive   │
│ ........................ │
│ AppleLink Package     ▶ │
│ BinHex4               ▶ │
│ btoa/atob             ▶ │
│ CPT Extract...          │
│ DDExpand...             │
│ DeArc...                │
│ MacBinary             ▶ │
│ Segmenting            ▶ │
│ tar                   ▶ │
│ Text Convert          ▶ │
│ UnPack...               │
│ UnZip...                │
│ UUCode                ▶ │
└─────────────────────────┘
```

Translating Foreign Archive Formats

StuffIt Deluxe can expand archives created with compression software other than a member of the StuffIt family. From the Macintosh, StuffIt can "translate" AppleLink packages, Compact Pro archives, and PackIt archives. From the PC, StuffIt can expand files that are in the Zip or Arc formats. Let's examine how to use each translator that can expand files from foreign archive formats. Unix tar archives are also able to be translated with StuffIt.

AppleLink Package (.PKG)

"AppleLink Package" is an external translator that lets you create and expand AppleLink packages without the AppleLink application itself. The "AppleLink Package" translator is available under the Translate menu. This is a hierarchical menu with choices of "Compress…" and "Expand…".

Compress…

Use the "Compress…" menu item to compress one or more files into an AppleLink package.

1. To compress selected files into an AppleLink Package, choose "Compress…" in the "AppleLink Package" hierarchical menu.

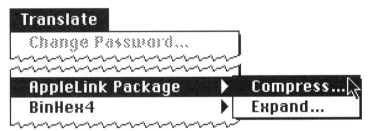

You will be presented with a modified standard file dialog which will allow you to select files and folders to compress.

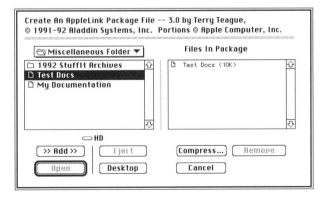

2. Use the "Add" button to add selected files and folders to the package.

You can open selected folders by clicking the Open button or double-clicking the folder name, or you can double-click files to add them.

The contents of the package will be displayed in the "Files in Package" list on the right. The expanded size of the folder or file will also be displayed. Double-clicking a selected folder opens or closes it.

Once a folder or file has been added to the package, the "Compress..." button is enabled to compress the package, or you can Cancel.

3. Select "Compress..." and you will be presented with a standard file dialog that will allow you to select the destination.

StuffIt adds a ".PKG" suffix to the name of the compressed file to indicate that it's an AppleLink package.

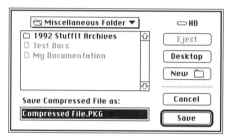

4. Click "Save" so the package will be compressed and saved to disk.

A progress dialog will be displayed as the files are compressed. When it's done, a dialog will be displayed showing you the savings made by compressing the files or folders into a package.

Expand...   Use the "Expand..." menu command to expand files from an AppleLink package file.

1. To expand the contents of an AppleLink package, choose "Expand" in the AppleLink hierarchical menu.

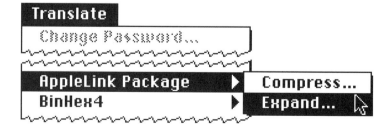

You will be presented with a standard file dialog which will let you select an AppleLink package to expand.

2. Select the package you want to open and click "Open" or press "Return".

The contents of the package will be opened and you'll be presented with an "Expand" dialog.

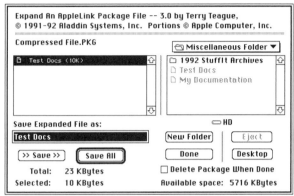

The contents of the package will be displayed in a list on the left-hand side of the dialog. If the package was created by a recent version of AppleLink (6.0 for example), the package's main window will contain hierarchical folders. Double-click a folder to show its contents; double click again to collapse it.

Selecting any folders or files allows you to save them to any spot on your hard disk. The dialog will show the amount of disk space that the expanded files will occupy and the current amount of free disk space on the destination disk. There is also a check box to automatically delete the package after it has been expanded and a button for creating a new folder.

3. To expand the selection(s), click "Save" or "Save All".

A progress dialog will be displayed as the files are expanded. If you clicked "Save", the AppleLink Package dialog will be presented again to select new files or folders until you click the "Done" button.

CPT Extract...

"CPT Extract..." is an external translator for use with StuffIt Deluxe and provides compatibility with the Compact Pro archive format. When the "CPT Extract" translator is installed, you can extract files in Compact Pro format. If the Compact Pro archive was encrypted or segmented, you won't be able to expand it.

1. **To extract a Compact Pro archive, choose "CPT Extract…" from the Translate menu.**

A dialog will appear, letting you select the Compact Pro archive that you want to extract from.

2. **Select the Compact Pro archive you'd like to extract and click "Open".**

A dialog will appear, indicating that StuffIt is opening the Compact Pro file and extracting the files.

UnZip… (.zip), DeArc… (.arc), UnPack… (.pit)

The "UnZip…", "DeArc…", and "UnPack…" translators all work in precisely the same way.

• The "UnZip…" command lets you expand files stored in the Zip format. Zip files are designated with a ".zip" suffix. Since a zipped file contains files on a foreign computer, you may not be able to use them on the Macintosh once they're unzipped. You must have an application that can use these files.

• The "DeArc…" command lets you expand files created with any of the numerous Arc programs and are designated by an ".arc" suffix. Just like Zip files, you may not be able to use the extracted files on the Macintosh because they were created on a foreign computer. You must have an application that can use these files.

• The "UnPack…" command lets you expand files created with the PackIt II and PackIt III compression utilities written by Harry Chesley. PackIt files generally have a ".pit" suffix. If the PackIt archive was encrypted, you won't be able to expand it.

1. To UnZip, DeArc, or UnPack a file, choose the proper command from the Translate menu.

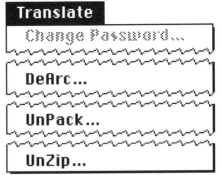

An Open dialog appears, letting you expand the file of your choice.

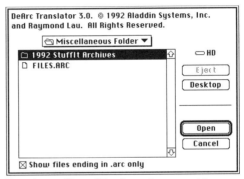

To only see files of the format you want to expand, check the "Show files ending in (.zip or .arc) only" check box and StuffIt will limit the items shown in the Open dialog.

Note: Since PackIt files were created on a Macintosh, all PackIt files will be listed in the Open dialog. Therefore, there is no check box for "…files ending in .pit…"

---

2. Select the archive you want and then click "Open".

StuffIt displays a dialog listing all the files that are stored within the archive.

3. Select the file or files you want to expand. To select more than one file, hold down the Shift key as you select them, and then click "UnZip", "DeArc", or "UnPack".

You can select multiple items by Shift-clicking or Command-clicking files in the list. Holding down the Shift key will extend the selection of files to the point where you clicked. If you hold down the Command key, you'll be able to add or remove individual items from your selection.

You may want to have the PC carriage return and linefeed "end-of-line" markers converted to the Macintosh-friendly carriage returns, using the "Convert CR/LFs to CRs" check box. Text files on the Macintosh use carriage returns to terminate lines.

4. StuffIt displays a dialog so you can save or convert the file(s).

• Clicking on the "Save" or "Save All" button expands the file(s) and saves it (or all of them) to disk.

- If you have a StuffIt archive open, the "Convert" and "Convert All" buttons convert the selected files in the foreign archive to StuffIt format and add them to the current archive. If you don't have a StuffIt archive open, the "Convert" or "Convert All" buttons will be dimmed.

- The "Skip" button lets you skip any file you are expanding.

- The "Cancel" button cancels the operation.

tar

The "tar" command lets you decode and encode files for use with the Unix tape archiver, tar. Many files available on Unix systems are archived with tar. Tar file names generally have a ".tar" suffix. This item has two sub-items: "Create…" and "Extract…".

Create…

The "Create…" menu item is used to build Unix tar files.

1. To begin creating a tar archive for transmission, choose "Create…".

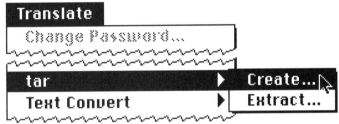

A dialog will appear, similar to the Stuff dialog. In this dialog, you add files or folders from the directory list on the left to the list of items to place into a tar archive on the right. A difference between this dialog and a Stuff dialog is the "Convert CRs to LFs" check box in the bottom of the dialog.

2. Select the files and folders to be archived.

You may want to select carriage returns to be converted to linefeeds, using the "Convert CRs to LFs" check box. Text files on the Macintosh use carriage returns to terminate lines. Unix systems use linefeeds to terminate lines so you may want to convert the carriage returns to linefeeds.

3. After selecting the files/folders, click "Archive All Items". You will be prompted to save the archive.

Note: When you transfer a tar archive from the Macintosh to another system, you should normally have the MacBinary option turned off in your file transfer program. Otherwise, the MacBinary header added by your file transfer program will prevent the archive from being recognized as a legitimate tar archive.

Extract...

Just as "Create..." is used to build tar files, "Extract..." is used to retrieve tar file contents.

1. To extract files from a tar archive, choose "Extract..." from the "tar" menu.

A standard Open dialog will come up letting you select the archive you'd like to extract.

2. Select the archive you want and click "Open".

When the archive opens, its directory will be read and displayed.

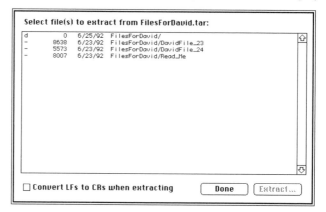

- If you just want to view the listing, select "Done" when you're finished. In the listing, the first column tells you whether something is a file, directory, or a special file (block, link, etc.). The symbol used is the same as that used by the Unix "ls -l" command.

- To extract files, select the files to extract using the Shift and Command keys to extend your selection if needed.

- If you want linefeeds (LFs) converted to carriage returns(CRs), check that check box before clicking the "Extract" button.

3. Click the "Extract" button.

You will be prompted for the location you want to extract the files/folders to. If there are any naming conflicts, you will be prompted whether to skip or replace existing files (with the option of replacing all future conflicting files). You may also cancel the process. Folders will never be replaced. This is in keeping with the Unix tar convention. Files will be placed into existing folders if folders have the same name.

Translating Different Data Formats

StuffIt Deluxe can translate other data formats to those readable by the Macintosh. These formats may or may not be compressed formats and are usually used for moving files between non-Macintosh computers. One translator lets StuffIt expand Macintosh DiskDoubler files. The others let you convert to and from formats (BinHex4, btoa/atob, MacBinary, UUCode, and Text Convert) that combine the complex Macintosh file into a simpler one for easy sending across networks. Let's look at each one in detail.

BinHex4

BinHex4 is a standard conversion algorithm used to convert Macintosh binary files to and from ASCII format. This format is primarily for transmission over networks that only support characters which can be typed from a keyboard, like Internet mail/news. On the Internet, BinHex4 is most commonly used on files that have already been Stuffed. If you do not already know about BinHex4, chances are that you do not require it. The "BinHex4" command has a hierarchical menu that lets you encode as well as decode files.

Encode...

The "Encode..." command lets you encode a file in BinHex4 format.

1. To encode a file to the BinHex4 format, choose the "Encode..." sub-menu from the "BinHex4" menu.

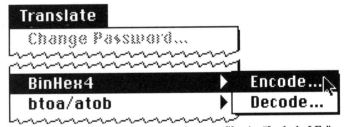

An Open dialog appears for you to choose a file. An "Include LFs" (linefeeds) check box at the bottom of the dialog is already checked by default.

The "Include LFs" option adds linefeeds to files. (On older computer systems, a linefeed causes the paper on a printer to advance to the next line without the carriage returning to the start of the next line.) In some environments, a BinHexed file may not be usable unless linefeeds are included with the normal carriage returns.

2. Select the file that you want to encode and click "Open".

StuffIt displays a Save dialog so you can rename the encoded file if you wish and select the folder you want to save it in. StuffIt automatically adds the ".hqx" suffix to the encoded file's name.

3. Click "Save" to encode the file in BinHex4 format.

StuffIt displays a progress dialog as it encodes the file.

Decode...   The "Decode..." command lets you decode a BinHexed file.

1. To decode a file from the BinHex format, choose "Decode..." from the "BinHex4" hierarchical menu.

A dialog opens for you to choose a file. A "Show files ending in .hqx only" check box is available at the bottom of the dialog and it is already checked for you.

2. Select the file that you want to decode and click "Open".

StuffIt displays a "Save" dialog so you can rename the decoded file if you wish and select the folder you want to save it in.

3. Within the dialog, click "Save" and StuffIt displays a progress window as it decodes the file.

If the decoded file is a StuffIt archive, a "Save & Open" button is enabled. Selecting it decodes the BinHex file and immediately opens the StuffIt archive.

btoa/atob   The "btoa/atob" (Binary to ASCII/ASCII to Binary) translator is an external translator that provides compatibility with the Unix programs "btoa" and "atob". Btoa and atob are Unix programs which convert 8 bit binary data to 7 bit ASCII data for transmission across channels which only support 7 bit ASCII data.

After you install this translator, you have a new choice under the Translate menu with the name "btoa/atob". This item has two sub-items: "Binary to ASCII..." and "ASCII to Binary...".

Binary to ASCII...   The "Binary to ASCII..." menu choice does the conversion of any Macintosh file to 7 bit ASCII.

1. **To convert a binary file to ASCII, choose "Binary to ASCII..." in the "btoa/atob" hierarchical menu.**

A dialog will appear letting you select the file you wish to convert to ASCII.

At the bottom of the dialog that appears is a check box labeled "Make MacBinary" checked by default. If you are encoding a Macintosh file, you should leave this checked. This will convert your file to MacBinary format before doing btoa translation. Unchecking this will eliminate information about your file, such as its type/creator.

2. **Select the file you wish to convert to ASCII format and click "Open".**

A Save dialog will appear, letting you save the ASCII document. To rename the document, simply type it in.

3. **Click "Save" and a progress dialog will come up, indicating that StuffIt is converting the file to ASCII format.**

ASCII to Binary...

When receiving a 7 bit ASCII file, you'll want to use the "ASCII to Binary..." menu choice to work with the file.

1) **To convert an encoded ASCII file to a binary file, choose "ASCII to Binary..." in the "btoa/atob" hierarchical menu.**

An Open dialog will appear, letting you select the file for conversion. The "Recognize MacBinary" check box at the bottom of the dialog will automatically be checked.

Normally, you should keep "Recognize MacBinary" checked. The translator will know when a file being decoded has been MacBinary encoded and when it hasn't. If you know the file was not from a Macintosh source or was not MacBinary encoded, then make sure this is not checked.

2. **Select the file you wish to convert to Binary format and click "Open".**

A dialog will appear letting you save the file to disk.

3. Click "Save" and a progress dialog will appear, indicating that StuffIt is converting the ASCII file and saving the file to disk.

DDExpand...

"DDExpand..." is an external translator for use with StuffIt and provides compatibility with the DiskDoubler files created by Salient. This translator requires that you have DiskDoubler installed in your system. If you try to use "DDExpand..." and DiskDoubler hasn't been installed, a warning dialog will appear telling you so.

1. To expand a DiskDoubler file, choose "DDExpand..." from the Translate menu.

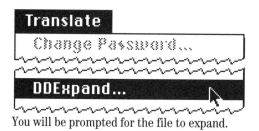

You will be prompted for the file to expand.

2. Select the file and it will be expanded.

MacBinary

The "MacBinary" translator is an external translator for use with StuffIt Deluxe that lets you "Encode..." or "Decode..." a file in MacBinary format for use in sending and receiving files to and from foreign computers across foreign networks. The "MacBinary" translator's main purpose is to combine the data and resource forks in these circumstances. MacBinary is sometimes referred to as BinHex5. Once installed, the "MacBinary" translator appears in the Translate menu.

Encode...

Use the "Encode..." menu choice to place files into MacBinary format.

1. To encode a file in MacBinary format, choose "Encode..." from the "MacBinary" hierarchical menu.

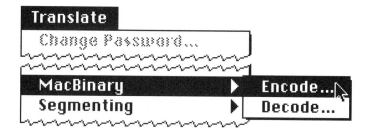

A standard Open dialog will appear letting you select the file you wish to encode.

2. Select the file you wish to encode and click "Open".

A Save dialog will appear, adding a ".bin" (for Binary) suffix to your file. To change the name, simply type the new name.

3. Click "Save" to encode the file.

A progress dialog will appear, indicating that StuffIt Deluxe is encoding the file in MacBinary format and saving it to disk.

Decode...

Use "Decode..." from the MacBinary menu to take a file out of MacBinary format back to a regular Macintosh file.

1. To decode a MacBinary file, choose "Decode..." from the "MacBinary" hierarchical menu.

A dialog will come up letting you select the file you wish to decode.

2. Select the file you wish to decode and click "Open".

A "Save" dialog will ask you where you want to save the file and if you want to rename it.

3. Name the new file, and click "Save" and the file with be decoded and saved to disk.

UUCode

The "UUCode" translator is an external translator for use with StuffIt Deluxe that lets you uuencode and uudecode files for use over Unix networks and computers. Once installed, the "UUCode" command appears in the Translate menu and it contains the uuencode and uudecode commands.

UUEncode...

"UUEncode..." is the encoding portion of the UUCode translator. Let's see an example of encoding a file.

1. To encode a file for use with a Unix network or computer, choose "UUEncode…" from the "UUCode" hierarchical menu.

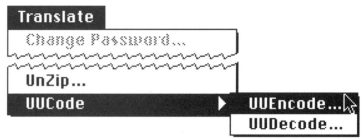

A dialog will appear letting you select the file to uuencode.

2. Select the file and click "Open".

A Save dialog will then appear letting you save the uuencoded file to disk. StuffIt automatically appends a ".uu" suffix to the file. To change the name, simply type it in.

3. Click "Save" to uuencode the file and save it to disk.

UUDecode…

When receiving a UUEncoded file, you need to use the "UUDecode…" menu command to work with that file.

1. To decode a uuencoded file, choose "UUDecode…" from the "UUCode" hierarchical menu.

A dialog will appear letting you select the file to decode. At the bottom of the dialog is a "Show only files ending in .uu" check box. Check this option if you want to only show files with the ".uu" suffix.

2. Select the file to decode and click "Open".

A dialog will appear with the default name for the file, minus the ".uu" suffix. To rename the file, simply type the new name now.

3. Click "Save" and the uudecoded file will be saved to disk.

Text Convert

The "Text Convert" Translator is used to convert text files for use on different types of computers. This is needed as different computers use different characters to specify the end of a line—the Mac uses a carriage return, Unix uses a linefeed, and the PC's uses both.

Convert to Macintosh

When receiving a text file from a PC or Unix computer, you'll want to use the "Convert To Macintosh…" menu command to have the line endings converted into those that are usable on the Macintosh.

1. Choose "Convert To Macintosh…" from the "Text Convert" hierarchical menu.

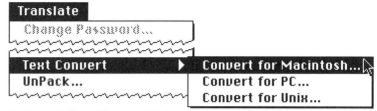

An Open dialog will appear letting you select the text file to convert.

2. Select the file to convert, and click "Open".

A dialog will appear with the name of the file with the suffix ".mac" appended to it. If you wish to use a different name, type it in.

3. Click "Save" to convert the file.

Convert to PC

When sending a text file to a PC, you'll want to use the "Convert To PC…" menu command to have the line endings converted into those that are usable on the PC. This will convert not only Macintosh files, but also Unix files for use on a PC.

1. Choose "Convert To PC…" from the "Text Convert" hierarchical menu.

A dialog will appear letting you select the text file to convert.

2. Select the file to convert, and click "Open".

A dialog will appear with the name of the file with the suffix ".pc" appended to it. If you wish to use a different name, type it in.

3. Click "Save" to convert the file.

Convert to Unix

When sending a text file to a Unix computer, you'll want to use the "Convert To Unix…" menu command to have the line endings converted into those that are usable with Unix.

1. Choose "Convert To Unix…" from the "Text Convert" hierarchical menu.

A dialog will appear letting you select the text file to convert.

2. Select the file to convert, and click "Open".

A dialog will appear with the name of the file with the suffix ".unix" appended to it. If you wish to use a different name, type it in.

3. Click "Save" to convert the file.

Segmenting

You may have noticed that the Translate menu also has a "Segmenting" command. Segmenting allows you to take very large files and split them into smaller pieces.

The "Segmenting" command is always available within StuffIt. Since it is integral to the software, it is not discussed in this chapter, but in "Chapter 4: Using StuffIt Deluxe."

Section Two: Magic Menu and Electronic Mail

Example: Mailing Archives on a LAN

Features Explained: Magic Menu's "Mail…" and "Stuff and Mail…"

Related Topic: See the section "Hooking up with the Finder and Magic Menu," beginning on page 137, in "Chapter 7: The Tools/Utilities."

Problem: You're on a Local Area Network (LAN) and you want to send files to others on the network. Is there an easy way to do this from the Finder?

Solution: Using Magic Menu and either CE Software's QuickMail or Microsoft Mail, you can "Mail" or "Stuff and Mail" files by simply selecting a menu item from Magic Menu.

Magic Menu is a control panel used to enhance StuffIt Deluxe. It lets you perform a variety of StuffIt functions from the Finder, including the ability to send files using electronic mail programs. Once you've installed Magic Menu, a Magic Menu icon will always appear in the Finder Menu bar. (See the section "Hooking up with the Finder and Magic Menu," beginning on page 137, in "Chapter 7: The Tools/Utilities" for an explanation of Magic Menu's other features.)

Three of the items in Magic Menu are pertinent to this chapter: "Mail Preferences...", "Mail...", and "Stuff and Mail...". We'll cover each in turn.

Mail...

The "Mail..." command lets you mail a single file to another user without having to use the application or desk accessory that came with your E-mail system. If you are not logged onto a mail server, the "Mail..." command will not be available.

1. To mail a file to another user from the Finder, select a single file icon and then choose "Mail..." from Magic Menu.

Magic Menu will automatically enclose the file in a QuickMail or Microsoft Mail document and present you with a list of users.

2. Select the user(s) you want to send the file to.

Consult your QuickMail or Microsoft Mail User's Guide for how to do this.

3. Type a message to be sent with the file enclosure and click "Send".

The file is enclosed and is sent to the user(s) you selected.

Alternate Method

■ If you hold down the Option key when choosing "Mail…", you'll get a dialog letting you set some temporary preferences.

Stuff and Mail…

The "Stuff and Mail…" command lets you Stuff one or more files and folders and mail them as an archive to another user in one operation.

1. To Stuff and send items to another user, select the files from any Finder window.

2. Choose "Stuff and Mail…" from the Magic Menu.

If you have selected one item, Magic Menu performs a Stuff on the selection and saves it to disk with ".sit" added to the end of its name. If you have selected multiple items, the archive will automatically be named "Archive.sit". You can check the "Ask for archive name" option (discussed on page 128) so that you'll always have an opportunity to name the archive to be sent.

3. Name the archive you're about to send and click "Save".

A progress dialog appears as Magic Menu Stuffs the selections.

When it's finished Stuffing, your E-mail memo window appears so you can address the archive to the recipient(s) and add a comment.

If a file with the same name already exists, Magic Menu prompts you to enter a new name for the file.

4. Select the user(s) you want to send the file to.

Consult your QuickMail or Microsoft Mail User's Guide for how to do this.

5. Type a message to be sent with the archive enclosure and click "Send".

The archive is enclosed and the message is sent to the user(s) you selected.

Alternate Method

■ If you hold down the Option key when choosing "Stuff and Mail…" from the Magic Menu, you'll get a dialog letting you set some temporary preferences for that one time you use the command.

Mail Preferences…

The Magic Menu "Mail Preferences…" command lets you set options for the "Mail…" and "Stuff and Mail…" commands as well as establishing which mail system to use.

1. Choose "Mail Preferences…" from the Magic Menu.

The "Mail Extension Preferences" dialog will appear.

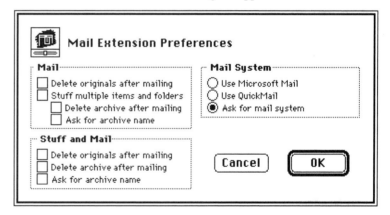

2. Set the Mail preferences you wish to use and click "OK".

The rest of this section explains these preferences in detail.

Mail

The "Mail" section of the "Mail Extension Preferences" dialog lets you set options for selecting files in the Finder and mailing them via Magic Menu.

Delete Originals After Mailing

Checking the "Delete originals after mailing" check box automatically deletes the original copy of the file after it is confirmed to be mailed.

Stuff Multiple Items and Folders	Checking the "Stuff multiple items and folders" check box lets you Stuff multiple items and folders at once. Once this option is selected, two other options become available to you.
Delete Archive After Mailing	Checking the "Delete archive after mailing" check box automatically deletes the local copy of the archive after you've mailed it.
Ask for Archive Name	Checking the "Ask for archive name" check box automatically brings up a standard Save dialog letting you rename the archive to be mailed. When this option is not checked, multiple selected items will be automatically Stuffed with the default name "Archive.sit" before they're mailed.
Stuff and Mail	The "Stuff and Mail" section of the "Mail Extension Preferences" dialog lets you set your options for selecting files in the Finder, and Stuffing and mailing them via Magic Menu.
Delete Originals After Mailing	If the "Delete originals after mailing" check box is checked, Magic Menu will automatically delete the original copy of the file selected in the Finder after it is confirmed to be mailed.
Delete Archive After Mailing	Checking the "Delete archive after mailing" check box automatically deletes the local copy of the archive after you've mailed it.
Ask for Archive Name	Checking the "Ask for archive name" check box automatically brings up a dialog to name the archive before it is Stuffed and sent. When this check box is not checked, Magic Menu uses the default "Archive.sit" name for the archive when Stuffing and sending.
Mail System	The "Mail System" portion of the preferences let you establish the default E-Mail software to use. If you are only using one mail system, Magic Menu will use the one you have installed.
Use Microsoft Mail	If the "Use Microsoft Mail" radio button is on, Magic Menu chooses Microsoft Mail as the default mail system to be used when sending files or archives using Magic Menu.
Use QuickMail	Selecting the "Use QuickMail" radio button chooses CE Software's QuickMail as the default mail system to be used when sending files or archives using Magic Menu.
Ask for Mail System	If both systems are available on your Mac, selecting the "Ask for mail system" radio button automatically prompts you for the E-mail system to use when sending files and archives using Magic Menu.

Section Three: StuffIt and Telecommunications

Introduction

Features Explained: Microphone II scripts and White Knight usage.

Related Topic: See "HyperCard XCMDs," beginning on page 168, in "Chapter 8: Automating StuffIt."

Two of the most popular telecommunication products are Software Ventures' MicroPhone II and FreeSoft's White Knight. We supply scripts that assist you in working with MicroPhone, and White Knight provides support from within the White Knight application.

Microphone II Scripts

StuffIt XCMDs are external code modules that can be attached to programs such as HyperCard from Claris Corporation and SuperCard from Aldus Corporation. In MicroPhone II, these commands let you Stuff and UnStuff files without leaving the program. The XCMDs are built into the "StuffIt Scripts" settings file, so all you need to do is open the settings from within the program to use the scripts.

1. To use the MicroPhone II scripts, launch MicroPhone II and choose "Open Settings…".

A standard Open dialog will appear, letting you open the "StuffIt Scripts" MicroPhone document.

2. Select the "StuffIt Scripts" file and click "Open".

When the StuffIt Scripts settings file opens, you'll notice four icons on the icon bar below the "StuffIt Scripts" window.

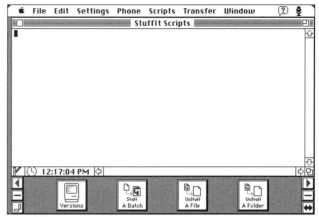

• Versions. Clicking this button displays the current version of the XCMDs.

• Stuff A Batch. Stuffing a batch is done by creating a listing of all the files you want to be Stuffed. MicroPhone will ask you to name the new archive. When you've told MicroPhone where it is, the Stuff XCMD takes over, Stuffing all the files in the batch. This is the batch dialog.

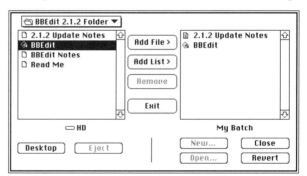

• UnStuff A File. You can UnStuff an archive by clicking the "UnStuff A File" button. A dialog will appear letting you rename the file if you wish, and asking you where you wish to put it UnStuffed.

• UnStuff A Folder. Clicking the "UnStuff A Folder" button lets you choose a folder that contains numerous archives that you wish to UnStuff all at once. A dialog will appear with the default folder name, asking you for a new name and location for the folder to be created. When you give the folder a new name, all the original archives are UnStuffed and placed in the new folder.

Note: To include StuffIt functionality in your own documents, use MicroPhone's Script Manager to export the scripts you wish to use. You should also move the XCMDs into your "MPToolBox" using ResEdit (or a similar tool).

White Knight

White Knight, from the FreeSoft Company, includes StuffIt Deluxe support right in the program so you can Stuff and UnStuff files without exiting White Knight. White Knight's scripting language also lets you create scripts to do this as well.

Stuff Files...

When you're ready to send files from within White Knight and they're not already Stuffed, you'll use White Knight's "Stuff Files..." command.

1. Begin by choosing the "Stuff Files..." command in the File menu.

A dialog will appear letting you select the Compression type (for older versions of StuffIt). Ignore these settings for StuffIt Deluxe 3.

2. Click "Select Files" or "Select Folders" depending upon what you want to Stuff.

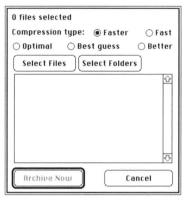

An Open dialog will appear, letting you select your file(s) or folder(s).

3. Select the item you'd like to Stuff in the dialog and click the "Select" button.

For each item you want sent, select it and click "Select". White Knight will add that item to its list of items to Stuff.

4. When you're done adding files, click "Cancel" to return to the Archive dialog.

The items you've selected will be listed in the window.

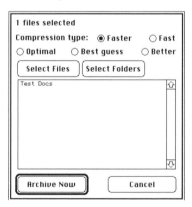

5. Click "Archive Now" to archive the files.

A Save dialog will appear with a default "Archive.sit" name selected for your archive.

6. To rename your file, simply type it in and click "Save".

A progress dialog will appear, indicating that StuffIt is archiving your file(s) from within White Knight.

UnStuff Files...

Once you download files from a remote service, you can use the "UnStuff Files..." command within White Knight. This way, you won't have to use SpaceSaver or the StuffIt application to UnStuff what you have received.

1. The first step is to choose "UnStuff Files..." from the File menu.

An Open dialog appears letting you select the file to be UnStuffed.

2. Select the archive you'd like to UnStuff and click "Select".

A dialog will appear letting you specify the folder to UnStuff to or rename the files you're about to UnStuff.

3. Click the "UnStuff" button to UnStuff the archive.

• If the archive contains more than one file, the "UnStuff All" button will be present and you can UnStuff all the files at once.

• If there is only a single file in the archive, the "UnStuff All" button will not appear, and you can simply UnStuff the file by clicking the "UnStuff" button.

• If the file name already exists, you'll be prompted to rename the file before it's UnStuffed.

Where To Go From Here

This concludes our discussion of the StuffIt network and communication extensions. You can continue to explore the other features of StuffIt by starting in any one of the following chapters or by taking a quick look at the Table of Contents for help in finding a topic you're interested in learning.

Chapter 7:
The Tools/Utilities

Introduction

StuffIt Deluxe comes with several Finder Extensions and Tools to provide alternate means for Stuffing and UnStuffing files and folders, as well as a converter to batch convert archives compressed with other formats, including older versions of StuffIt. You can pick and choose among these tools, depending upon your style of work. Though these shortcuts don't provide you with the same features you get with the StuffIt Deluxe application itself, they sometimes offer quicker ways of getting things done.

In this chapter, we explain how to use the Drop Boxes, portions of Magic Menu, StuffIt Converter™, and the StuffIt XTND.

Hooking up with the Finder and Drop Boxes

Example: Stuffing with Drop•Stuff

Feature Explained: Drop•Stuff.

Related Topics: See "Example: UnStuffing with Drop•UnStuff" starting on page 136; the Magic Menu "Stuff" command, beginning on page 140; and "Chapter 3: Using StuffIt SpaceSaver."

Problem: You'd like to send a file to your friend in another city over an online service, but the file is 100K and will take too long to send. What's a quick way to Stuff the file into an archive?

Solution: Drag the file onto the Drop•Stuff icon in the Finder.

Note: Drop Boxes can be used with System 7 only. A Drop Box is a very small application that is able to perform tasks by "dragging and dropping" items onto them. Since only System 7 supports "drag and drop" features, Drop Boxes will not work for System 6 users.

Drop•Stuff   Drop•UnStuff

Drop•Stuff and Drop•UnStuff are incredibly easy to use. You can use them right where they are, or you can drag them to the Desktop where your hard drive and Trash icons are located. This lets you use them whether a specific folder in the Finder is open or not. We recommend that you move the two drop boxes to the Desktop, though you can put them anywhere you like.

1. From the Finder, select the file(s) you want to Stuff and drag them on top of the Drop•Stuff icon on the desktop. When the Drop•Stuff icon is highlighted, release the mouse button.

Drop•Stuff Stuffs the file(s) in the same folder (or on the Desktop) as the original, leaving a copy of the original UnStuffed file.

If an archive with that name already exists, or if you hold down the Shift key when dropping a file or folder onto the Drop•Stuff icon, a dialog will appear asking you to rename the new archive.

Note: Holding down the Option key when using Drop•Stuff will have Drop•Stuff delete the original item(s) when they are successfully Stuffed into an archive. Holding down the Shift key when using Drop•Stuff will have a dialog appear that provides you with additional options such as "Make Self-Extracting Archive".

Alternate Methods

■ Two other alternate methods for stuffing files in the Finder are to either use Magic Menu's "Stuff" command (see the next section in this chapter, "Magic Menu") or to attach the ".sit" suffix to any file or folder (see "Chapter 3: Using StuffIt SpaceSaver").

Example: UnStuffing with Drop•UnStuff

Feature Explained: Drop•UnStuff.

Related Topics: See "Example: Stuffing with Drop•Stuff" starting on page 135; the Magic Menu "Expand" command, beginning on page 138, and "Chapter 3: Using StuffIt SpaceSaver."

Problem: You log onto your favorite bulletin board system to download some utilities and you notice that they have file names with ".sit" suffixes attached to them. These are StuffIt files that were Stuffed before they were put up on the bulletin board. After you download them, you have to UnStuff them before you can use them. What's the easiest way to do this?

Solution: Use the Drop•UnStuff box in the Finder.

1. Select the StuffIt archive you downloaded from the bulletin board and drag its icon onto the Drop•UnStuff drop box.

Drop•UnStuff will UnStuff the archive and a place the UnStuffed items in the same folder as the original archive.

• If the archive contains multiple items, a new folder (with the name of the archive) will be created and everything will be UnStuffed into the new folder.

• If a file with that name already exists (minus the ".sit" suffix), a dialog will appear asking you to rename the file.

Note: Holding down the Option key when using Drop•UnStuff causes Drop•UnStuff to delete the original archive(s) after they are UnStuffed.

Alternate Methods

■ Select the archive and choose "Expand" from the Magic Menu. See the next section in this chapter, "Magic Menu" for details.

■ Remove the ".sit" extension from any StuffIt archive. See "Chapter 3: Using StuffIt SpaceSaver," beginning on page 19, for details.

Hooking up with the Finder and Magic Menu

Example: Point & Click Stuffing from the Finder

Features Explained: Magic Menu, Stuff, Compress, Expand, Make Self-Extracting, Preferences, and About Magic Menu.

Related Topics: See "Chapter 3: Using StuffIt SpaceSaver" and "Chapter 4: Using StuffIt Deluxe." See "Chapter 6: Network/Communication Extensions," "Section Two: Magic Menu and Electronic Mail," beginning on page 124, for information on using Magic Menu's Mail, Stuff and Mail, and Mail Preferences commands.

Problem: Every day you manage files and folders in the Finder, using any number of StuffIt's and SpaceSaver's features: Expanding (SpaceSaver files or StuffIt archives), Stuffing archives, compressing for transparent access, or making Self-Extracting archives. How can you do these everyday tasks without having to run the StuffIt application?

Solution: "Magic Menu" lets you accomplish these tasks from the Finder.

Magic Menu is a control panel that's installed when you install StuffIt Deluxe. It extends some of StuffIt's abilities to the Finder by adding a menu to the Finder's menu bar.

Note: On some systems, the word "Magic" appears in the Finder's menu bar, instead of the Magic Menu icon shown in this User's Guide.

We're going to confine our description here to the main commands that are enabled by Magic Menu.

Expand

The "Expand" command (Command-U) lets you expand any selection of icons from the Finder. This command works with SpaceSaver files, StuffIt archives (.sit or .sea), Compact Pro archives (.cpt), and AppleLink packages (.PKG). Here is how to use "Expand" to UnStuff an archive.

1. To expand archives, select one or more archives in the Finder.

2. Choose "Expand" (Command-U) from the Magic Menu.

Magic Menu performs an "Expand" on the archive and saves the file to disk using the name of the archive, minus the ".sit" suffix.

If the name chosen for the expanded file or folder already exists, a dialog will appear, letting you rename the expanded item.

Alternate Method

■ If you hold down the Option key when choosing "Expand..." from Magic Menu, you'll get a dialog letting you set some temporary preferences. Follow these steps to see how it's done.

1. **After selecting one or more items, hold down the Option key when you choose "Expand", Magic Menu displays a dialog with additional options.**

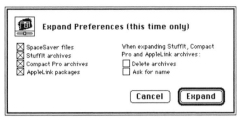

These check boxes are the same as the options found in the "Expand" section of the Magic Menu Preferences. See "Expand Preferences," beginning on page 142, for details.

2. **Simply check or uncheck the options you want and click the "Expand" button.**

If you want to cancel the entire operation, click "Cancel".

Compress

The "Compress" command lets you compress selected files and folders using SpaceSaver.

1. **In the Finder, select one or more items that you want to compressed.**

2. **Choose "Compress" from the Magic Menu.**

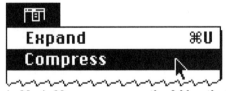

As Magic Menu compresses the folder, the SpaceSaver status indicator will show that Magic Menu and SpaceSaver are hard at work.

Note: This spinning StuffIt cursor is the default progress indicator for SpaceSaver. It is also possible to instruct SpaceSaver (and therefore the Magic menu "Compress" command) to display full progress dialogs or no progress indicator at all. These preferences are explained in "Chapter 3: Using StuffIt SpaceSaver" under the heading "Status Display" on page 30.

For more information on SpaceSaver (and its interaction with Magic Menu), see "Chapter 3: Using StuffIt SpaceSaver."

Alternate Method

■ You can rename a file or folder and attach the SpaceSaver keyword to compress it.

Stuff

The "Stuff" command (Command-S) lets you Stuff files and folders without using the StuffIt Deluxe application.

1. To Stuff a file, select one or more items in the Finder and then choose "Stuff" from the Magic Menu.

Magic Menu Stuffs the file and saves it to disk as a StuffIt archive. A progress dialog appears as Magic Menu Stuffs the file.

If a file with the same name already exists, Magic Menu prompts you to enter a new name for the file.

Alternate Method

■ If you hold down the Option key when choosing "Stuff…" from the Magic Menu, you'll get a dialog letting you set some temporary preferences.

These check boxes are the same as the options found in the "Stuff" portion of the Magic Menu Preferences. See the section "Stuff Preferences," beginning on page 143, for information on each option.

Make Self-Extracting

The "Make Self-Extracting" command in Magic Menu makes a self-extracting archive out of any selected items in the Finder.

1. **To create a self-extracting archive, select one or more items in the Finder and choose "Make Self-Extracting" from the Magic Menu.**

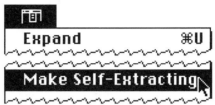

Magic Menu will Stuff the file(s) or folder and attach a ".sea" suffix to the resulting archive. The default name for the self-extracting archive will be the name of the file or folder, or "Archive.sea".

If the name of the self-extracting archive already exists, Magic Menu will prompt you to rename the archive.

Alternate Method

■ If you hold down the Option key when choosing "Make Self-Extracting…", you'll get a dialog letting you set some temporary preferences.

These check boxes are the same as the options found in the "Make Self-Extracting" portion of the Magic Menu Preferences. See the section "Make Self-Extracting Preferences," beginning on page 144, for information on each option.

Magic Menu Compression Preferences

When you installed the software, some basic Magic Menu preferences were preconfigured to make compression and expansion with Magic Menu effortless. You can change these preferences to better use the Magic Menu commands available to you. These preferences can be found in the Finder by choosing "Preferences…" (found just under the Make Self-Extracting command) from the Magic Menu.

After choosing "Preferences…", you'll see the Magic Menu Compression Extension Preferences dialog.

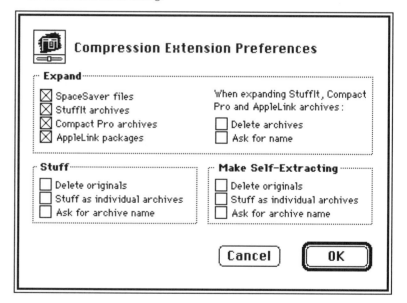

Expand Preferences

There are a few preferences that specifically address what happens when you expand any type of file from the Magic Menu.

SpaceSaver Files

The "SpaceSaver files" check box enables Magic Menu to expand, or decompress, files that have been compressed with StuffIt SpaceSaver. You may choose to turn this option off if you do not want Magic Menu's "Expand" command to work on "small" files. This option is checked on initial installation of the software.

StuffIt Archives	If you have the "StuffIt archives" option checked, Magic Menu will expand, or UnStuff, any StuffIt archives when choosing "Expand" from the Magic Menu. StuffIt files are archives that are recognizable because they usually have ".sit" at the end of the file name. You might want to turn this option off if you want the "Expand" command to not UnStuff StuffIt archives. This option is checked on initial installation.
Compact Pro Archives	The "Compact Pro archives" check box does the same as the "StuffIt archives" check box, but it expands Compact Pro archives instead. Compact Pro is an archiving software product. A Compact Pro archive is identifiable by a file name that usually ends with ".cpt". The default for this check box is on.
AppleLink Packages	The "AppleLink packages" check box does the same as the "StuffIt archives" check box, but it expands AppleLink archives, which are usually called packages. AppleLink is Apple Computer Inc.'s telecommunications software that can create archives, or packages. An AppleLink package is identifiable by an file name that usually ends with ".PKG". The default for this check box is on.
Delete Archives	The "Delete archives" check box tells Magic Menu to delete the original archives just after they're expanded. This is very useful for clearing archives off your disk when the expanded software is ready for your use. This check box is preconfigured to be off.
Ask for Name	The "Ask for name" check box lets Magic Menu bring up the standard Macintosh directory dialog for each archive to be expanded. When this dialog appears, you can change the name of files being extracted, or save them to a different folder or disk. This check box is not checked when the software is installed.

Stuff Preferences

The Stuff options in the Preferences dialog lets you set the functionality for the Magic Menu "Stuff" command.

Delete Originals	Using the "Delete originals" check box will have Magic Menu delete all original files after they're placed into archives. This check box defaults off.
Stuff as Individual Archives	If you check the "Stuff as individual archives" option, Magic Menu will place every selected item into multiple archives when Stuffing. If this check box is off, as it is preconfigured, whatever's selected when you choose "Stuff" will be combined into one archive.
Ask for Archive Name	The "Ask for archive name" is a simple, self-explanatory check box. Turning it on has Magic Menu ask you for the name of the new archive, instead of automatically naming it. With this option checked, a directory dialog will appear so that you can save new archives in any folder or disk you want. This check box is not checked when SpaceSaver and Magic Menu are installed.

Note: The default name of an archive that contains multiple items is "Archive.sit". Using Magic Menu's "Stuff" command on a single item will create an archive using that item's name. If you will usually be Stuffing multiple items, you might want to set the "Ask for archive name" preference so that you always have an opportunity to name the new archives.

Make Self-Extracting Preferences

The "Make Self-Extracting" command in Magic Menu turns any selection into a double-clickable application. It is the same as attaching ".sea" to any file or folder name and is most useful for sending software to people who don't own any StuffIt software. The "Make Self-Extracting" options in the Preferences dialog set the functionality for the Magic Menu "Make Self-Extracting" command.

Delete Originals

Using the "Delete originals" check box will have Magic Menu erase all original files after they're placed into a self-extracting archive. This check box is preconfigured unchecked.

Stuff as Individual Archives

If you check the "Stuff as individual archives" check box, you'll have Magic Menu place every selected item into multiple self-extracting archives. If this check box is off, as it is preconfigured, whatever is selected when you choose "Stuff" will be combined in a single self-extracting archive.

Ask for archive name

The "Ask for archive name" option forces Magic Menu to ask you for the name of the new archive, instead of automatically naming it. With this option checked, you can also automatically save the archive in any folder or disk you want. This option is not checked when the software is first installed.

Note: The default name of an self-extracting archive that contains multiple items is "Archive.sea". Using Magic Menu's "Make Self-Extracting" command on a single item will create a self-extracting archive using that item's name. If you'll be making self-extracting archives that contain multiple items on a regular basis, you might want to check the "Ask for archive name" check box so that you always have an opportunity to name new self-extracting archives.

About Magic Menu...

"About Magic Menu…" displays a dialog that provides version information and credits for Magic Menu.

When you choose "About Magic Menu...", a dialog will appear, showing the authors, your name, version number, and address and phone number of Aladdin Systems.

StuffIt Converter

Example: Converting Older Archives

Feature Explained: StuffIt Converter.

Related Topic: See "Convert 1.5.1 Archives to 3.0 on Open" on page 86 in "Chapter 4: Using StuffIt Deluxe".

Problem: You have archives that have been compressed with an older version of StuffIt and you'd like to convert them to StuffIt Deluxe 3 format to take advantage of better compression and some of the new features of the program. How do you do this?

Solution: You use StuffIt Converter and accomplish the task all at once.

StuffIt Converter is an application which will aid you in converting your older StuffIt archives, as well as other types of archives into the new StuffIt format in order to squeeze even more space out of archives. StuffIt Converter works on BinHex files (.hqx), StuffIt archives (.sit), Compact Pro archives (.cpt), AppleLink Packages (.PKG).

StuffIt Converter can be used in two ways.

System 7 Only

If you are running System 7, you can drag individual archives, or entire folders or disks onto the StuffIt Converter icon. StuffIt Converter will launch and proceed to expand the contents of the original archive. Once expanded, the original archive will be deleted, and a new archive with the same, original name will be created and the expanded contents will be Stuffed into the new StuffIt archive. This will happen for all items that are dragged onto StuffIt Converter.

Note: Using StuffIt Converter on BinHex files will cause them to be decoded from BinHex format, UnStuffed, and encoded into BinHex.

System 6 or Batch Mode

If you are using System 6, or have a number of archives you want to convert, you'll want to use the "batch" mode of StuffIt Converter. Here is a tutorial for batch conversions.

1. From the Finder, double-click on StuffIt Converter application to open it

StuffIt Converter will display its "batch list" where you can add archives that you want to convert.

2. Click "Add..." to add an archive to the list of files to be converted.

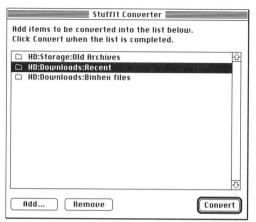

An Open dialog will appear, asking you which individual BinHex files, StuffIt archives, Compact Pro archives, AppleLink Packages, or folders or disks you wish to add to the list of files to be converted.

3. Select a file, folder, or disk and click "Add".

Unlike most Open dialogs, after clicking "Add" you'll still find yourself in the Open dialog, allowing you to add other items to the StuffIt Converter "batch list." If you have more items to add to the list, repeat this step.

4. Click "Done" to exit from the dialog and return to the StuffIt Convert "batch list" window.

If you accidently added something you didn't want to add, you can select the item(s) and click the "Remove" button to remove the item(s) from the list.

5. Click "Convert".

You'll see the progress of the conversion process displayed in a series of standard StuffIt progress indicators.

Once all the conversions have taken place, StuffIt Converter is ready to perform more conversions, or you may use "Quit" in the File menu to exit StuffIt Converter.

StuffIt XTND

Example: Using On Location to Know About Files Within Archives

Feature Explained: StuffIt XTND.

Related Topics: None.

Problem: You're using On Technology's On Location, a program which enables you to index your whole hard disk for quick file searches, but you'd also like to know what files you have in your StuffIt archives. What do you do?

Solution: Using the StuffIt XTND, you're able to index the files within archives almost as easily as you indexed regular files using On Location.

Note: The StuffIt XTND only finds the names of files within archives and not the text within the Stuffed items.

Claris Corporation has devised file conversion mechanisms for its software called XTNDs. XTNDs are also used by other software developers to utilize foreign file formats without reinventing the wheel. Today, using the XTND technology, users of Claris's MacWrite II or other programs can simply choose "Open…" to access files created on IBM-PCs or by other programs. Using this XTND, products compatible with it can quickly determine the contents of an archive.

Note: This example assumes you are working with On Location 2.0 or later.

---

1. To use the StuffIt XTND with On Location, simply place it inside the Claris folder found within the System Folder.

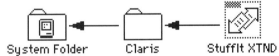

System Folder   Claris   StuffIt XTND

The installation of a XTND-compatible product always creates a Claris folder within the System folder.

2. Open the "On Location" Desk Accessory from the Apple menu.

The On Location Desk Accessory menu and window will appear on the screen.

3. Choose "Create Index..." in the On Location menu.

A Create Index dialog will open.

4. Select the disk you have StuffIt archives on and click the "Custom..." button.

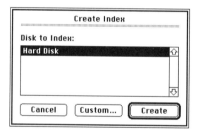

5. In the "Create Custom Index..." dialog click the "Specify File Kinds..." dialog.

We need to do this since StuffIt archives are not normally indexed with On Location.

6. **In the "Specify File Kinds" dialog, scroll down the "Don't Index…" list (on the right) until you see the three StuffIt listings. Double-click on each one to add them to the "Index these files" list on the left.**

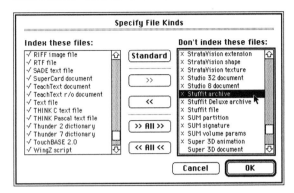

Note: From now on, every index you create from scratch, on any disk, will index the file names within StuffIt archives.

7. **Click "OK" to close the dialog.**

You'll find yourself back in the "Create Custom Index…" dialog.

8. **Click "Create" to create a new index.**

If you have already indexed that disk in the past, you'll get a dialog asking if you want to replace the existing index. You must create a new index from scratch in order to use the StuffIt XTND.

Once an index is created on one or more disks, you'll want to locate the file names of items within StuffIt archives. This is easily done.

1. **Open the "On Location" Desk Accessory from the Apple menu, if it is not already open.**

2. **Click the "Text in File" radio button and type any portion of the name of the file you want On Location to look for inside of StuffIt archives.**

In this example, we're looking for a letter written to Paul Cannon, but we're not sure when it was written and what archive it's in.

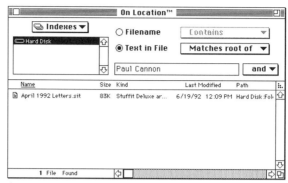

On Location displays "April 1992 Letters.sit" in the window as an archive that contains a file whose name contains "Paul Cannon".

3. Double-click on the file name shown in the On Location list.

On Location will open a window containing a view of the archive contents. Now that you know which archive has the document you need, you can exit On Location and UnStuff the archive.

Where To Go From Here

This completes the chapter on StuffIt Deluxe's Tools and Utilities. If you haven't explored other chapters, you can do so now—see the Table of Contents for assistance in finding a topic you're interested in. If you're following these chapters in sequence, you might want to turn now to "Chapter 8: Automating StuffIt" to learn how to automate StuffIt with its built-in scripting language or with other software such as QuicKeys 2, MPW, and HyperCard.

Chapter 8:
Automating StuffIt

Section One: Scripting Within StuffIt

Introduction

StuffIt's scripting language allows you to automate many of StuffIt's operations. You can create a script in any text editor or word processor, provided you save the file in text format. You can also use the "Record Script" command to create a script.

In another part of this User's Guide, "Chapter 10: Scripting Reference," beginning on page 175, there is a listing of all scripting commands, including some not explained in the following tutorials.

Example: Scripting Your Monthly Archive

Features Explained: Record Script, Execute Script, and Edit Script Menu

Related Topics: See the tutorials in "Section Two: Beyond the Basics," beginning on page 53, in "Chapter 4: Using StuffIt Deluxe." Also see the two examples, "Example: Scripting Your Yearly Archive," beginning on page 160, in this chapter.

Problem: You know that archiving and backing up your files on a regular basis is a wise practice, but you find it tedious, especially when you're backing up your drive to floppies. How do you automate your everyday archiving and backup strategies, making them as painless as possible?

Solution: You script your monthly archiving process with StuffIt Deluxe. Then, using your word processor, you edit the script to modify the criteria by which files are Stuffed.

Before we can proceed with this example, you need to have the Script menu available in StuffIt's menu bar. See "The StuffIt Menus," on page 89, for setting those preferences.

1. In this example, we've organized our hard drive by application folders. In them, we place each application with all its related files.

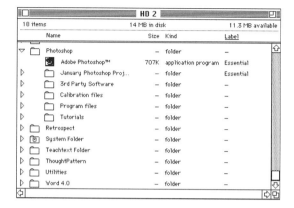

2. Next, we create a project folder within our application folder. In our example we use a Photoshop folder called "January Photoshop Projects".

You can use any application you want.

3. We've also created a folder within our StuffIt Deluxe Folder called "1992 StuffIt Archives".

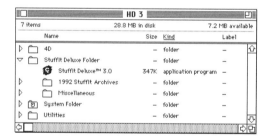

4. Finally, if your Script menu isn't active, turn it on by choosing the "Preferences…" command in the Edit menu.

5. When the "Preferences…" dialog appears, check the "Script" menu check box in the "Menus" area and click "OK".

Recording a Script

As mentioned, we can create scripts from scratch with a word processor or text editor. An easier way is to use "Record Script…" (Command-R) and put

StuffIt into a "watch me" mode where it will generate script commands for each and every action you do until you tell it to stop recording the script.

1. Choose "Record Script…" (Command-R) from the Script menu.

A dialog will appear asking you to name the script.

2. Name the script "Photoshop Script" and click "Save".

StuffIt saves the script to disk and goes into "Record" mode, indicated by the blinking tape recorder in the Apple menu. "Record" mode will stay on until you choose "Stop Recording" at the end of this example.

3. Choose "New" (Command-N) from the File menu.

A dialog will appear asking you to name the new archive

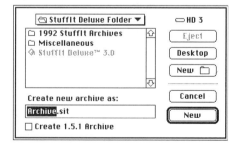

4. Name it "Photoshop Projects.sit" and click the "New" button.

StuffIt will save the new archive to disk.

5. Choose "Stuff" from the Archive menu.

The "Stuff" dialog will appear.

6. Go to the Photoshop folder, open it to select the "January Photoshop Projects" folder, and add it to the "Items to Stuff" list by selecting the folder and clicking the "Add" button.

7. When the folder moves to the list on the right, click the "Stuff" button (Command-S).

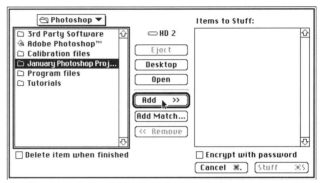

StuffIt will Stuff the folder into the "Photoshop Projects.sit" archive.

8. When StuffIt is finished, close the archive and choose "Stop Recording" (Command-R) from the Script menu.

StuffIt automatically generates a script in Text format named "Photoshop Script". To read the script, open it within a word processor or text editor.

```
; StuffIt Deluxe Script (v3)
Write Status To
New Archive "HD 3:StuffIt Deluxe Folder:Photoshop
  Projects.sit" replace
Use "Photoshop Projects.sit"
Stuff "HD 2:Photoshop:January Photoshop
  Projects:" compress
Close "Photoshop Projects.sit"
```

At this point, you could add the script to StuffIt's Script menu by choosing the "Add Script…" command from the hierarchical "Edit Script Menu".

You could also assign this new menu item a Command key equivalent. At a stroke, your January Photoshop Projects folder would be automatically Stuffed into a "Photoshop Projects.sit" archive every time you executed the command.

Before you add it to your menu, though, you might want to edit it. Think for a moment:

• Do you want to add a new "January Photoshop Projects" folder to your "Photoshop Projects.sit" archive every time you execute the script, instead of replacing the earlier copy with a new one? By changing a single line in the script, you can create an "audit" trail of past versions of your files.

• Do you want to add only those files which have been modified that week to the archive? Later, we'll show you how StuffIt Deluxe's new "Add Match" feature lets you select criteria such as "last week," date modification ranges, or other criteria, to back up your files by.

• Do you want to archive just your January Photoshop Projects, or do you want to archive the January files for any application on your drive?

• Do you want to save this archive to a floppy rather than your hard drive?

Editing a Script

We're going to change the script to back up to a floppy instead of the hard drive, and add a "Quit" command to quit StuffIt Deluxe after Stuffing the folder. First, let's examine the script.

1. Begin by creating a floppy diskette named "January Photoshop Floppy".

2. Open the newly created script within a word processor or text editor.

```
(1) ; StuffIt Deluxe Script (v3)
(2) Write Status To
(3) New Archive "HD 3:StuffIt Deluxe
    Folder:Photoshop Projects.sit" replace
(4) Use "Photoshop Projects.sit"
(5) Stuff "HD 2:Photoshop:January Photoshop
    Projects:" compress
(6) Close "Photoshop Projects.sit"
```

Note: We placed line numbers in front of each script line to make them easy to refer to. A real script would not show these numbers.

This "Photoshop Script" was automatically generated by StuffIt. It's a typical script, with each command beginning a new line and with the argument and modifiers following the commands in quotes.

Line (1) is a header for the script. The semicolon (;) before the line marks it as a comment, and the line is not executed.

Line (2) writes a "status file" to disk once the script has been executed, giving it the name of the script plus a ".out" suffix. One status file gets written per script. If you add a name to the end of the "Write Status To" line, the ".out" file will also have that name. This status file is used to help you debug your scripts. If you don't want a status file, remove line (2).

Line (3) creates the archive. The long string between quotes is the pathname to the archive. We'll change this line for backup to a floppy.

3. Eliminate the path designations "`HD 3:StuffIt Deluxe Folder:`" prior to "`Photoshop Projects.sit`" in line 2 and replace them with "`January Photoshop Floppy:`"

Now, when the script is run, it will create the archive on the "January Photoshop Floppy" disk instead of on the hard drive.

Since we're examining the script, let's continue looking at each line in detail.

First, be aware that Line (3) does one more thing: every time it creates the archive, it writes over any older version of the archive that it finds at the end of the drive path by means of the "replace" command at the end of the line.

Note: If you changed "New" to "Open" at the beginning of the line, and removed the "replace" command, StuffIt would open the "Photoshop Projects.sit" archive every time the script is run and would Stuff a new version of the "January Photoshop Projects" folder into the archive. In this way, you could create an audit trail of your changing projects folder, but the archive could get very big.

Line (4) isolates the archive to use. The "`Use`" command is used to make a specific archive active when you have multiple archives open.

We'll leave the next two lines alone. Line (5) Stuffs the Photoshop folder and compresses it and line (6) closes the archive.

4. Add another line after the Close command line, a "`Quit`" command that will quit StuffIt after the script is run.

5. Save the changes (making sure it's still a Text file).

Now the script reads as follows:

```
Write Status To
New Archive "January Photoshop Floppy:Photoshop
  Projects.sit" replace
Use "Photoshop Projects.sit"
Stuff "HD 2:Photoshop:January Photoshop
  Projects:" compress
Close "Photoshop Projects.sit"
Quit
```

Executing a Script

How can we be sure that the changes we made work? We'll use the "Execute Script…" command to check it. Once we see that it's OK, we'll add it to the Script menu and give it a command key equivalent so it can be executed with a single menu selection or keystroke.

1. Choose "Execute Script…" (Command-E) from the Script menu.

A dialog will appear, letting you select the script for execution.

2. Select "Photoshop Script" and click the "Execute" button or type "Return" or "Enter" on your keyboard.

StuffIt will execute the "Photoshop Script". It will create a new archive on your January Photoshop Floppy and call it "Photoshop Projects.sit". It will Stuff your January Photoshop Projects folder into the archive, close the archive when it's done Stuffing, and quit StuffIt.

Adding a Script to the Menu

Now that we've tested it, let's add it to the Scripts menu and give it a Command key.

1. Choose "Add Script…" command from the "Edit Script Menu".

A dialog will appear letting you select the script to add to the menu.

2. Select "Photoshop Script" and click the "Add" button or type the "Return" key on your keyboard.

The "Photoshop Script" menu command will appear at the bottom of the Script menu.

3. **Give it a Command key by choosing "Assign Command Keys..." from the "Edit Script Menu" hierarchical menu.**

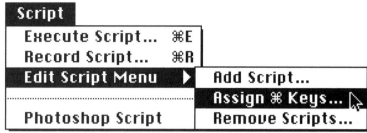

A dialog will appear letting you select the script and assign a Command key to it.

4. **Select the "Photoshop Script" and type the Command key sequence you want and click "OK".**

If the Command key you chose has already been assigned, a dialog will appear telling you so. If this is the case, you should select another Command key.

The Command key equivalent will be added to the "Photoshop Script" menu item.

Removing a Script from the Menu

Of course there will be times when you will want to remove a script from the StuffIt menu. Doing so is just as easy as adding a script to the same menu. Follow these 2 steps to do this.

1. Choose the "Remove Scripts…" sub-menu from the "Edit Script Menu".

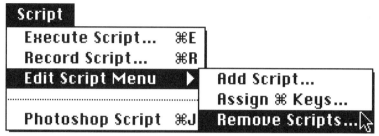

A dialog will appear, letting you select the script for removal.

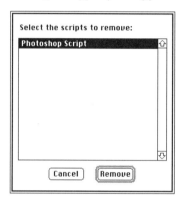

2. Select the script(s) you want to remove and click the "Remove" button or type "Return".

To select more than one script for removal, hold down the "Shift" key as you select additional scripts.

The script(s) will be removed from the Script menu.

Example: Scripting Your Yearly Archive

Features Explained: Record Script, Add Match Scripting

Related Topics: See the previous tutorial, "Example: Scripting Your Monthly Archive." Also see the tutorials in "Section Two: Beyond the Basics," beginning on page 53, in "Chapter 4: Using StuffIt Deluxe."

Problem: Now that you've gotten your feet wet on a simple StuffIt script for everyday backups, how do you create a single, yearly archive for archiving your month-to-month work?

Solution: Using StuffIt's "Add Match" feature in conjunction with "Record Script…" you archive all your files across project folders into one yearly archive.

1. **Choose "Record Script…" (Command-R) from the Script menu, and when the Script dialog appears, name the script "1991 Yearly Script".**

2. **Choose "New…" (Command-N) in the File menu to create a new archive and name it "1991 Yearly Archive.sit".**

3. **Choose "Stuff" (Command-S) from the Archive menu, or click on the Stuff icon in the Archive palette.**

   The "Stuff" dialog will appear, letting you select the files and folders you'd like to add to your archive.

4. **Click on the "Desktop" button to let you choose among the hard disks to backup onto.**

5. **Select the hard drive you want to back up and then click on the "Add Match…" button in the "Add Match" file dialog.**

   The Add Match Criteria dialog will appear, letting you select what to add to the archive by a number of criteria.

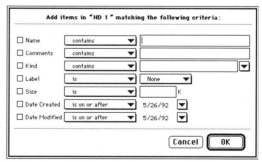

Notice here that by selecting more criteria you narrow the number of files matching all your criteria. For purposes of this experiment, the only criteria we're going to use is to select all files that have been modified "Last Year".

6. Select the left "Date Modified" pop-up menu that reads "is on or after" and change it to the "is between" option.

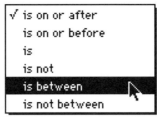

The "is between" command activates a third pop-up menu for the "Date Modified" options.

7. Select the "last year" command in the middle "Date Modified" pop-up menu.

8. Choose "this year" in the right "Date Modified" pop-up menu.

The "Date Modified" check box will automatically be checked, indicating that any file modified between 1/1/91 and 1/1/92, will be included in the archive.

9. Click "OK" and you'll return to the "Stuff" file dialog.

Notice how "HD 1" has been added to the "Items to Stuff" list, with small
lines in the icon, indicating that only some of the files in that volume will
be Stuffed.

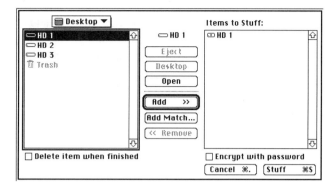

11.Click the "Stuff" (Command-S) button.

StuffIt will scan your drive for all files that have been modified last year
and will Stuff them into the "1991 Yearly Archive" along with the folders
they're in.

12. When StuffIt's done adding the folders and files, click the close box on the archive.

13. Choose "Stop Recording..." (Command-R) from the Script menu.

Our 1991 Annual Script will look like the following, minus the numbers which
we've added for purposes of this example.

```
(1) ; StuffIt Deluxe Script (v3)
(2) Write Status To
(3) New Archive "HD 3:StuffIt Deluxe Folder:1991
    Yearly Archive.sit" replace
(4) Use "1991 Yearly Archive.sit"
(5) Clear Match
(6) Match Modified 1/1/1991 to 1/1/1992
(7) Stuff "HD 1:" match compress
(8) Close
```

Let's look at a few lines here that we've never explored before. Line (5) clears
the Match command (clearing any previous matches), and line (6) Modifies
Match by telling StuffIt to only Stuff files that have been modified between 1/
1/91 and 1/1/92. Line (7) actually Stuffs the files on hard drive "HD 1",

matching our criteria, compressing them as they're Stuffed. Line (8) closes the archive.

14. Add "`Quit`" (without brackets) on a (9)th line, and StuffIt will quit after executing the command.

Remember that this script can be easily modified by changing the dates in line (6) to any range you like. That way, if you only want to add the past month's changes to the yearly archive, all you need to is to put the past month's date range in that line and only those files modified within the past month will be Stuffed into your yearly archive.

Alternate Method

■ Scripts can be written that use criteria such as "today," "yesterday," "this week," and "last week" as well as specific date ranges. Scripts using "today" or "yesterday" use the Macintoshes internal clock to "stamp" the date criteria onto the operation.

Where To Go From Here

The scripting language is comprehensive and allows you to script almost every StuffIt Deluxe feature. The best way for you to begin scripting is just as we have done in this chapter: use the "Record Script…" command and edit your new script further to suit your needs. All of the scripting language commands and their syntax is covered in detail in "Chapter 10: Scripting Reference" which starts on page 175. If you'd like to learn how to automate StuffIt Deluxe without the scripting language, read on.

Section Two: Automating StuffIt From Outside

Introduction

StuffIt Deluxe not only lets you automate the archiving process from within StuffIt itself– you can automate the compression process without using StuffIt's scripting language.

CE Software's QuicKeys 2, Apple Computer's MPW, or Claris' HyperCard can be used with the externals we provide to Stuff or UnStuff files in those respective products.

Using the powerful System 7 mechanism of Apple events, StuffIt Deluxe can be 'remote controlled' by other products that are able send Apple events to StuffIt. This is also known as Inter-Application Communications. Userland Frontier and Simple Software's Control Tower are other examples of applications that provide remote scripting of StuffIt.

Apple events

Apple events are messages sent from one application to another. They're sent to request a service ("Please perform this task"), to respond to a request ("I've done what you asked; here's the result") or to send news ("Here's something you might want to know"). Apple events can also contain data, and therefore they are also used to move data from one application to another.

StuffIt Deluxe supports a large number of Apple events, which give you the ability to control and automate many of the capabilities of the product. The most common usage of this will be via a scripting systems such as UserLand Frontier, though some specific application, such as a communications software, may also call upon StuffIt to perform some tasks for it.

In order to facilitate your use of StuffIt with scripting systems, StuffIt includes an 'aete' resource which details the full compliment of Apple events supported. A complete Frontier Verb Table is also included on disk for users of UserLand Frontier. StuffIt Deluxe is also prepared for the future of Apple events, and many of its functions are recordable by an Apple event recorder when one becomes available.

In addition to being controlled, StuffIt will also use the Finder itself to open and launch files when you use the Launch command. StuffIt Deluxe will also use Apple events in conjunction with Anti-Viral software to scan your newly UnStuffed files for possible infection. See "Detect Viruses With…," beginning on page 87, in "Chapter 4: Using StuffIt Deluxe" for setting the preference in the StuffIt application.

If you are a developer, and wish to get more specific information about the Apple events that StuffIt supports, contact Aladdin Systems at (408) 761-6200 or on AppleLink at ALADDIN.

QuicKeys 2

Example: Using Macros to Automate Archiving

Features Explained: The Stuff and UnStuff QuicKeys 2 extensions.

Related Topics: None.

Problem: You use QuicKeys 2 from CE Software to automate many of your daily activities, from launching programs to backing up files. How can you link StuffIt Deluxe into your automated backup process, using archives instead of just files and folders?

Solution: Using the QuicKeys extensions provided with StuffIt Deluxe, you fully automate your archival process.

QuicKeys 2 is a popular macro program from CE Software that can record your actions and replay them by typing a keystroke. When you purchase QuicKeys 2, Aladdin's Stuff and UnStuff extensions are automatically installed along with QuicKeys 2 and are ready to be used. With QuicKeys 2 and the StuffIt Extensions, you can establish as many Stuff/UnStuff macro variations as you wish, from backup sets that can be invoked each time you startup your Macintosh, to single keystrokes that ask you what files to compress.

This example assumes that QuicKeys 2 is installed on your Macintosh.

The Stuff Extension

1. Begin creating a Stuff QuicKey by opening QuicKeys 2.

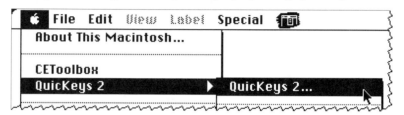

This can be done with the QuicKeys 2 hierarchical menu or with a preconfigured keystroke (usually Command-Option-Return).

2. Choose "Stuff" from the Extensions sub-menu.

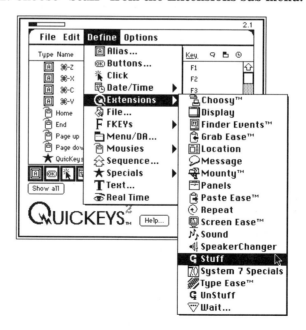

The Stuff Extension dialog will appear, with the extension "Stuff" already named. You can change the name if you wish.

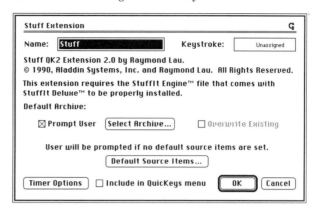

3. **Press Tab to move to the "Keystroke:" field. Type in the keystroke you'd like to assign to the "Stuff" QuicKey.**

4. **Select the options you'd like and click "OK".**

The Stuff Extension lets you specify two general options:

• The archive to Stuff into (Select Archive...)

• The items to be Stuffed (Default Source Items...)

With the first option, you can have QuicKeys always prompt you for the archive name, or click on the "Select Archive" button to specify the name of a new archive that is to be used. The "Overwrite Existing" option will have the Stuff Extension replace an old archive with a new one, should it already exist on disk.

The "Default Source Items..." button brings up a dialog that is similar to the Stuff dialog with the StuffIt Deluxe application. Here, you can set up a consistent set of files that you always want archived. If no items are specified, QuicKeys 2 will ask you for the files each time it is invoked.

The other options in the dialog are standard QuicKeys 2 options and are described in the QuicKeys 2 User's and Extensions Guides.

The UnStuff Extension

1. **To create an UnStuff QuicKey, open QuicKeys 2 and choose "UnStuff" from the Extensions sub-menu.**

The UnStuff Extension dialog will appear, with the extension "UnStuff" already named. You can change the name if you wish.

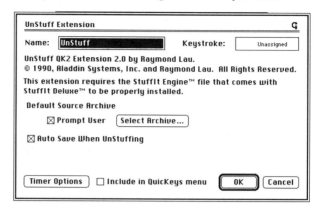

2. Press Tab to move to the "Keystroke:" field. Type in the keystroke you'd like to assign to the "UnStuff" QuicKey.

3. Select the options you'd like and click "OK".

The UnStuff Extension lets you specify whether a designated archive is to be UnStuffed (using the "Select Archive…" button) or whether you should be prompted each time for the archive to be UnStuffed on disk. You can also elect to automatically save your UnStuffed files to disk.

The other options in the dialog are standard QuicKeys 2 options and are described in the QuicKeys 2 User's and Extensions Guides.

HyperCard XCMDs

HyperCard, from Claris Corporation, has its own type of external modules called XCMDs. These externals are also supported by a few other applications such as SuperCard by Aldus Corporation, Plus from Spinnaker, and MicroPhone II from Software Ventures to name just a few. We have included XCMDs with StuffIt Deluxe so that these applications (and others that support XCMDs) can have compression abilities added to them.

We supply you with two separate XCMDs: Stuff and UnStuff. These XCMDs allow you to both create StuffIt Deluxe archives and UnStuff any StuffIt archive.

We supply the HyperCard XCMDs inside a HyperCard stack called "StuffIt XCMDs". It's a fully-working stack that you can use to find out more about our XCMDs and test them as well.

To place the Stuff and UnStuff XCMDs in your own stacks, you need to use a resource copier such as ResCopy or ResEdit. Once these XCMDs are in your own stack, they're part of the HyperTalk language and can be accessed like any other command. If using HyperCard 2.0 and later, you can also use the "using "StuffIt XCMDs""command in a stack to take advantage of these XCMDs without resource copying.

The Stuff XCMD has the following syntax:

```
Stuff archiveName, fileList [makeSEA] [delete]
```

archiveName is a full pathname (including path and filename) for the new archive you want created. fileList is a container of carriage-return (<CR>) delimited list of files and folders to be archived. You may optionally use the MakeSEA parameter to create a self-extracting archive instead of a regular StuffIt archive. You can also optionally use delete parameter to delete the original items after they are Stuffed into an archive.

The UnStuff XCMD has the following syntax:

```
UnStuff archiveName [destination] [delete]
```

archiveName is a full pathname for the archive you want UnStuffed. If there are multiple items in the archive, the contents of the archive are placed into a new folder called "archiveName Folder". You can optionally use the destination parameter to specify another pathname to place the UnStuffed items. The delete parameter may also be used to delete the archive after everything is UnStuffed from it.

MPW Tools

The Macintosh Programming Workshop (MPW) is a development environment from Apple Computer for writing software for the Macintosh. Like StuffIt Deluxe, it has an open architecture where new modules may be added at any time. Since many programmers use StuffIt Deluxe in their daily archiving, we now include MPW Tools that can be integrated into any MPW script. Users of MPW should move the two StuffIt MPW tools (Stuff and UnStuff) into their MPW Tools folder. If you do not use MPW, you should trash the "StuffIt MPW Tools" folder since you don't need them.

Both MPW tools are commando-compatible, so typing "Stuff…." or "UnStuff…." will bring up a commando dialog. Within that dialog, all parameters are fully explained and help is available there for further information.

Chapter 9: UnStuffIt

Introduction to UnStuffIt

UnStuffIt is an application that allows you to expand files that have been Stuffed, compressed, or segmented with any StuffIt product including StuffIt Lite, StuffIt Deluxe, and StuffIt SpaceSaver.

UnStuffIt is termed a freeware product. This means that you may give it away to your friends, family, or anyone you please, as long as you don't charge for it or distribute it with a commercial product. If you'd like to distribute it with a commercial product, contact Aladdin Systems and we'll arrange for you to do so. **It is the only part of this package that you may freely copy and give away.**

Installation

UnStuffIt is not installed on your machine with an Easy Install. In order to install UnStuffIt, you must use the Installer to do a Custom installation. See "Custom Installation" on page 19 of "Chapter 2: Installation" for a tutorial on doing a custom installation.

We did not install UnStuffIt on your disk because you will never need to use it—it is only useful for distribution to your friends. It is placed in a self-extracting archive to make it convenient for you to give it to others. At any time, you can copy the self-extracting archive to another disk and give it to anyone.

Example: Opening SpaceSaver Files within UnStuffIt

Feature Explained: Expanding SpaceSaver files from within UnStuffIt.

Related Topic: See "Chapter 3: Using StuffIt SpaceSaver."

Problem: You've taken a presentation you've compressed with SpaceSaver to a client's location, but discover that your client does not have SpaceSaver.

Solution: Double-click the file anyway. If your client has a copy of either StuffIt Deluxe, StuffIt Lite, or UnStuffIt, that application will launch and proceed to decompress the file. You can then open the document with your application.

Note: If your client does not have a StuffIt product, give them a copy of UnStuffIt. Once your client has UnStuffIt, you can give them SpaceSaver files and StuffIt archives.

Alternate Method

■ It is also possible to decompress a SpaceSaver file or UnStuff an archive by opening the UnStuffIt application and choosing "Expand" from the File menu.

Note: You may also notice that when SpaceSaver is turned off from the control panel, any compressed files will now have StuffIt icons instead of the ones that you normally see.

Example: UnStuffing from StuffIt Archives

Feature Explained: Expanding StuffIt archives from within UnStuffIt.

Related Topics: See "Chapter 3: Using StuffIt SpaceSaver," "Chapter 4: Using StuffIt Deluxe," and "Chapter 7: The Tools/Utilities."

Problem: You're going to be sending a large number of StuffIt archives to a friend (who doesn't have a StuffIt product) over the modem and do not wish to make each one a self-extracting archive. How do you send StuffIt files and have your friend UnStuff them?

Solution: Send your friend the UnStuffIt application once and have them use UnStuffIt to UnStuff the archives you send. This is done using the "Expand…" command within UnStuffIt. Once your friend chooses this command, he/she needs to select the archive to be UnStuffed and its contents will be saved to disk.

Example: Joining Segmented files

Feature Explained: Joining files from within UnStuffIt.

Related Topic: See the tutorial "Example: Backing Up Your Yearly Archive," beginning on page 61, in "Chapter 4: Using StuffIt Deluxe."

Problem: You need to send a friend a segmented archive (who doesn't have a StuffIt product). How do you send your friend segmented files and have your friend join them together?

Solution: Send your friend the UnStuffIt application and have them use UnStuffIt to join the segmented file together and UnStuff the archive you sent. Your friend will first have to use the "Join" command from UnStuffIt's File menu. He/she will be prompted for the first segment to join. Once your friend specifies each segment, UnStuffIt will continue joining the segments until it is done. Once the large archive is together, your friend can use the "Expand…" command in the File menu and UnStuff the archive.

More about UnStuffIt

UnStuffIt has a few other features that you may wish to take advantage of:

• "About UnStuffIt", in the Apple menu, will display information about the authors of the product and which version you are currently using.

• To exit the program, choose "Quit" from the File Menu.

Chapter 10:
Scripting Reference

Introduction

StuffIt's scripting language allows you to automate many of StuffIt's operations. You can create a script in any text editor or word processor provided you save the file in text format. You can also use the "Record Script" command in StuffIt Deluxe to create a script automatically for you.

Scripting Rules

• Each "Line" in a script must end with a carriage return. You insert a carriage return by typing the Return key.

• Each command must appear as a separate line.

• Each line must not be longer than 255 characters. These 255 characters include the command, its parameters (including pathnames and filenames), and a carriage return. You will find other references to carriage returns in this section referred to as «cr».

• All references to disks, folders, or files must be within quotes.

• A colon (:) must be used to designate a disk or folder name. For example, "Big Man:" refers to a disk while "Big Man" refers to a file. When a disk name is followed by one or more folders and a colon is the last symbol in this group of characters, the entire group (including the colon) is called a "pathname."

• A filename consists of a pathname followed by the name of the file and is used to refer to a file on a disk. An itemname, which is just the name of the file or folder, is used to refer to an entry within an archive.

• When a command takes two filenames or pathnames (such as "rename file"), the first is considered the source and the second the destination or target.

• Comment lines begin with a single dash (–), two dashes (– –), or a semi-colon (;). They are ignored by StuffIt. StuffIt also ignores any blank lines.

• Commands are not case sensitive. Letters within scripts may be upper or lowercase. This includes script commands and the names of disks, folders, and files. This chapter lists commands in all lowercase characters for reading convenience.

Throughout this reference section, you'll notice certain symbols used to help you understand the syntax of a command. These symbols should not be used literally. Any word that is within < > specifies a required substitution where you would replace it with appropriate text. For example, in the case of "`<command>`", the command "Stuff" may be used. Square brackets [ ] enclose optional elements which may be included if you need them to expand the meaning of the command. In the case of "`new archive <filename> [replace] [1.5.1]`", the words "`replace`" and "`1.5.1`" are both optional. Each modifies the command "new archive" to do different things. Helper words, enclosed by « », aren't required by StuffIt but help make the command more readable by you. The next section, "Helper Words" lists the words that can be used. Words on either side of the separator character | are used in an either/or situation. For example, "`Apple|bat|car`" calls for only one of the three words to be used.

Scripts have a simple syntax in which the command is the first element in a line. It is followed by the argument (the archive or filename), and the two elements are separated by a space as in:

```
<command name> <space> <argument> <cr>
```
Thus, a script for Stuffing a file would be:

```
New Archive "Hard Disk:The King.sit"
Stuff "Hard Disk:Large File"
Close Archive "The King.sit"
```
Any of StuffIt's options can be added after the argument.

```
<command name> <space> <argument> <space>
  <options> <cr>
```
To delete the original file in the previous example, add a "delete" option to the end of the line.

```
Stuff "Hard Disk:Large File" delete
```

Helper Words

These "helper words" may be used within certain script commands to enhance readability. They aren't required for a script command to function but help make descriptions more readable for you and others who will read the script after you. Within a command description, suggested helper words are surrounded by « ». The "Record Script" command does not generate these helper words.

ago	existing	security
and	finished	segments

as	from	than
at	in	using
compression	into	when
done	is	with
encryption	secure	

Wildcards

StuffIt's scripting language supports two wildcard characters: the question mark (?) and the asterisk (*). The question mark matches any single character. The asterisk matches none, one, or more characters.

If you need to use a question mark, an asterisk, or a quoatation mark in a script, enter a backslash \ before the character. This causes StuffIt to treat the character literally. For instance, if you have used an asterisk or question mark in a filename, you would use "*" to match the "*" or "\?" to match "?". Also, "\\" matches "\" and "\"" matches a single quotation mark.

When you are using wildcards to specify items in an archive, all matching is done at the root level of the archive. You can use wildcards to match both files and folders.

When you are specifying files and folders on a volume, wildcards are allowed in the file or folder name portion of the command line. If the command matches a folder name, the folder is treated as one entity when it's Stuffed.

You can also use an asterisk as a substitute for the entire volume name. To include all of the files named "ReadMe" on all volumes at the root level only, your script should contain:

```
*:ReadMe
```
Likewise, an asterisk can be used as a substitute for any filename. To include all files whose names end in ".pnt" in your graphics folder on the volume named Hard Disk, you would enter:

```
Hard Disk:Graphics:*.pnt
```
A question mark wildcard is used to match a single character in a volume, folder, or filename. Among other uses, this can be used to archive a series of files that ends with a different suffix. To include all files (use asterisk) that have a single character (use question mark) after a period on the root of the volume named "HD" you would use:

```
HD:*.?
```
As shown, wildcards can be used individually or in combination with other wildcard characters.

Variables

StuffIt's scripting language supports five special variables, whose value is evaluated each time the script is run much like variables in a traditional programming language, that you can include in your scripts. Variables must be enclosed in { } to differentiate them from standard text and are most commonly used as part of another text string (such as a pathname).

The five variables supported in StuffIt are:

`{Date}`, today's date,

`{Time}`, the current time,

`{Startup}`, the name of the startup (or boot) disk,

`{System}`, the pathname to the system folder, and

`{Deluxe}`, the pathname to the folder where StuffIt Deluxe is located.

A common use of this would be "`write status to "{Deluxe}status file"`".

The Scripting Commands

`abort on error`

The "Abort on Error" command is used to tell StuffIt what to do when a script encounters an error. Using this command will cause StuffIt to simply abort the entire script after an error is encountered. This will override the default setting which is to continue on errors.

To cause StuffIt to abort a script when it finds an error, enter this line near the beginning of your script.

```
abort on error
```

`clear match`

The "Clear Match" command is used to clear out any match criteria that may have been previously set. It is a good idea to use this before setting up any new match criteria in a script.

To clear any existing match criteria, enter this line in your script:

```
clear match
```

`close archive [<filename>]`

The "Close Archive" command closes an open archive. Use this command whenever you want to close an archive. If you do not specify an archive, the current archive is closed. It is always a good idea to specify the archive to avoid any ambiguity.

To close the archive "The King.sit" when you've finished Stuffing some files into it, enter the line,

```
close archive "The King.sit"
```
in your script. If "The King.sit" is the only archive open, you can omit its name.

`continue on error`

The "Continue on Error" command is used to tell StuffIt what to do when a script encounters an error. Using this command will cause StuffIt to continue executing the rest of the script, even after an error is encountered. This is the default setting, but you can use it after the use of the "abort on error" command to revert to this setting.

To reset StuffIt to continue a script when it finds an error, enter this line in your script:

`continue on error`

`decode binhex`
`<filename> [«to»`
`<filename>]`

The "Decode BinHex" command decodes a BinHexed file. BinHex is a standard conversion algorithm used to convert Macintosh binary files to ASCII format.

To decode a BinHex file, enter the line,

`decode binhex "Hard Disk:The King.hqx"`
in your script. StuffIt will decode the BinHex file "The King.hqx". If you specify a target pathname, the decoded file will be placed in that folder with the name stored in the BinHex file. If you include a filename instead, then that name will override the one stored in the original file. If the target name cannot be used, StuffIt will not decode the file and will give you an error message in the status file.

`delete entry`
`<itemname>`

The "Delete Entry" command deletes entries from an archive. It deletes all entries at the root level of the archive matching the specified itemname. Use this command to delete an entry from an archive that you no longer need or when you are going to replace it with a newer version.

To delete an entry, enter the line,

`delete entry "My File"`
in your script. The entry is immediately deleted from the archive.

`delete file`
`<filename>`

The "Delete file" command deletes individual files from the specified disk. For safety reasons, no wildcard substitutions are allowed. To delete a file, enter the line,

`delete file "Hard Disk:My File"`
in your script. The file is immediately removed from the disk.

`destination`
`<pathname>`

The "Destination" command lets you set a new destination for files that StuffIt UnStuffs from an archive. Use this command when you want to save files to a different folder, hard disk, or diskette.

Specify the destination by entering the pathname. For instance, you would enter the name of your hard disk in quotation marks if you wanted to save the UnStuffed files to the root level. If you want to save the files to a folder on your hard disk, you would enter the name of the hard disk followed by a colon, and then the name of the folder. This would appear as:

```
"Hard Disk:New Files:"
```
To set a new destination, enter the line,

```
destination "Hard Disk:New Files:"
```
in your script

```
encode binhex
<filename> [«to»
<filename>] [«with»
LFs] [replace]
```

The "Encode BinHex" command encodes a file in the BinHex format. If you are transmitting the file over a network (such as the Internet) that doesn't support the Macintosh binary format, you will need to convert the file to the BinHex format first.

If you do not specify the name of the encoded file, StuffIt assumes you want to name it "<source filename>.hqx" with the "source filename" being the original name of the file. If you want the BinHexed file to have a specific name, you can enter that name.

To encode a file in BinHex format, enter the line,

```
encode binhex "Hard Disk:The King.sit"
```
in your script. To add linefeeds to the file as it is encoded and specify an alternate destination you might enter the line:

```
encode binhex "Hard Disk:The King.sit" to "Floppy
   Disk:TheKing.hqx" with LFs
```

```
join <filename>
[prompt] [replace]
```

The "Join" command lets you join files which have been segmented. The Join command does not normally require you to respond to the join process and will automatically join segments in a single folder. If you wish to be able to insert diskettes, or if the segment names do not end in sequence (".1", ".2", ".3", etc.) you must use the "Prompt" option. Using the "Prompt" option causes StuffIt to bring up a dialog asking for more information. The "Replace" option will cause StuffIt to overwrite an existing file with the same name as the file being joined if one exists.

To join a file, enter the line,

```
join "Hard Disk:The King.sit.1"
```
in your script.

```
launch <itemname>
```

The "Launch" command lets you launch a file contained in an archive. This is a shortcut to doing an "UnStuff" and then a "Transfer", if the file you wish to launch is contained in an archive. When running System 6, you can only launch applications, however with System 7 any file can be launched.

To launch a file, enter the line,

```
launch "The King"
```
in your script.

`match <category>` `<comparison> <value>`	The "Match" command is used to specify a set of criteria to be applied to the next "Stuff match" operation. Each "Match" command is added to a list of criteria, so you can have multiple criteria applied, just like the "Add Match" dialog. For more info on "Add Match", and the list of categories, comparisons, and values see "Close-up: The Add Match Dialog," beginning on page 81, in "Chapter 4: Using StuffIt Deluxe."

To match all files labeled as "project," enter the line:

```
match label is "Project"
```
To match all files ending in .c modified this week, enter the lines,

```
match name ends with ".c"
match modified this week
```

`new archive`
`<filename> [replace]`
`[«as» 1.5.1]`
	The "New Archive" command allows you to create a new archive and open it for use.

To create a new archive, enter the line,

```
new archive "Hard Disk:The King.sit" replace
```
in your script. The "Replace" option causes StuffIt to replace any existing file with the same name. If you do not specify that StuffIt should replace an archive with the same name, StuffIt will put up a dialog asking if the archive is to be replaced. If you do not respond to this dialog (within 20 seconds), it does not create a new archive and does not run the remainder of the script.

The "1.5.1" option lets you create a StuffIt 1.5.1 archive, which is an older and less efficient format. You would not normally want to create a 1.5.1 archive. If you do not specify "1.5.1" in the script, StuffIt creates a standard archive.

To create a StuffIt 1.5.1 archive and replace any existing file with that name, enter the line,

```
new archive "Hard Disk:Old Archive.sit" as 1.5.1
  and replace
```
in your script.

`new folder <pathname>`	The "New Folder" command allows a new directory to be created on any disk. The pathname must designate the location and name of the new folder to be created. Once a new folder has been created, it can be used in subsequent script commands.

To create a folder at the root level of the disk "Hard Disk" enter,

```
new folder "Hard Disk:My Folder"
```
in your script.

`no status`	The "No Status" command stops any output of diagnostic information following a "Write Status To" command.

To stop outputting diagnostic information, include the command:

```
no status
```

`open archive`
`<filename>`

The "Open Archive" command allows you to specify an archive for StuffIt to open. Use this command if you want to add files to an existing archive.

To open an archive, enter the line,

```
open archive "Hard Disk:The King.sit"
```
in your script.

`quit`

The "Quit" command exits StuffIt. It has the same effect as selecting "Quit" from the File menu.

To quit StuffIt, you would enter the line,

```
quit
```
at the end of your script.

Even though your script may end with the "Transfer" command, to exit StuffIt and run another program you may want to put a "Quit" command at the end of any scripts that run unattended. This would ensure that even if the Transfer command fails, StuffIt will still quit.

`rename entry`
`<itemname> «to»`
`<itemname>`

The "Rename Entry" command allows you to rename items within an archive. Use this command if you want to rename an entry before a file with the same name is added to the archive.

To rename an archive entry, use the line,

```
rename entry "Large King" to "Large King Backup"
```
in your script.

`rename file`
`<filename> «to»`
`<filename>`

The "Rename File" command allows you to rename a file on the hard disk. Use this command if you want to rename a file to avoid a naming conflict.

To rename a file, use the line,

```
rename "Hard Disk:Archive.sit" to "Hard Disk:The
   King.sit"
```
in your script.

`save as <filename>`
`[«as» self-`
`extracting]`
`[replace]`

The "Save As" command allows you to save an archive under a different name, and optionally as a self-extracting archive. Using the "Replace" option, you can also have StuffIt replace an existing file which might be in the same location.

To save an archive as a self-extracting archive, use the line,

```
save as "Hard Disk:Archive.sit" as self-
   extracting
```

`segment <filename>`
`<size|max> [prompt]`
`[replace]`
	The "Segment" command allows you to split a file into multiple segments. Without the "Prompt" option, StuffIt will create the segments with sequential suffixes (".1", ".2", ".3", etc.) and will save them to the same folder as filename. If you wish to rename segments or place the segments on diskettes as the script is running, you must specify the "Prompt" option. You can also specify the "Replace" option if you want StuffIt to overwrite any existing files with the same names.

To segment a file, enter the line

`segment "Hard Disk:The King.sit" 775K`
in your script. This instructs StuffIt to split the file "The King.sit" into 775K segments. The "K" is optional when specifying the segment size. You can also use "max" to specify the maximum size. When segmenting a file for diskettes, remember to allow room for the diskettes directory. In other words, you may not be able to fit a segment larger than 775K on a double-sided (or 800K) diskette. The directory on the diskette requires several kilobytes of free disk space. |
| `stuff`
`<pathname\|filename>`
`[none\|compress]`
`[encrypt] [delete]`
`[match]` | The "Stuff" command adds a file or folder to the currently selected archive. Use this command whenever you want to add files or folders to an open archive. When adding the files or folders, you may also specify if they are to be compressed or encrypted. You must have an open archive for the "Stuff" command to work.

To Stuff a file or folder in the current archive, enter the line,

`stuff "Hard Disk:Large File" delete`
in your script. In this case, the file "Large File" is compressed into the current archive and the original file is deleted after the file is compressed. If the file is not successfully Stuffed, it is not deleted.

Rather than simply specifying a single file, or an entire folder, you can use the "Match" option to have the current set of match criteria applied. It is just like doing it from the "Add Match" dialog. For example, if you had some match criteria set, you might add this to your script:

`stuff "Hard Disk:My Folder:" match` |
| `stuff «in» place`
`<pathname\|filename>`
`[«as»1.5.1]`
`[none\|compress]`
`[encrypt] [delete]` | The "Stuff in Place" command will create a new archive (called <pathname\|filename>.sit) and Stuff the specified files or folders into it. When Stuffing the files or folders, you may also specify if they are to be compressed or encrypted, or if the archive to be created is an 1.5.1 archive. If you are just going to be creating single file/folder archives, this is much faster than doing a "New Archive", "Stuff" and "Close Archive" for each.

To Stuff a file or folder in the current archive, enter the line,

`stuff in place "Hard Disk:Large File" delete` |

in your script. In this case, the file "Large File" is compressed into its own archive called "Large File.sit" and the original file is deleted after the file is compressed. If the file is not successfully Stuffed, it will not deleted.

```
transfer
<application>
```

The "Transfer" command quits StuffIt and transfers to the specified program. Use this command if you want to return to a program after running a script. For example, you might want to return to your word processor after executing a script to archive the day's work.

If StuffIt cannot find the program, the script continues its execution. The "Quit" command should follow the "Transfer" command if the script is executed unattended.

To run a program, enter the line,

```
transfer "Hard Disk:Applications:TeachText"
```
in your script.

```
translate
<translatorName>
BEGIN
<Encode|Decode>
<filename> <«to»
filename|pathname>
END
```

The "Translate" command is used to control the plug-in translators via scripting. With it you can have any translator encode files intoor decode files from foreign formats. Unlike the other scripting commands, the "Translate" command allows you to specify a group of commands to the translator by bracking the group with BEGIN/END. Between the BEGIN/END, you may specify an number of encoding or decoding commands, along with any translator specific commands that may be available. For example, many of the translators support the "LF" command for specifying the inclusion or translation of linefeeds.

To expand all the files from a Compact Pro archives, use the line,

```
translate "Compact Pro"
begin
decode "HD:Downloads:*.cpt"
end
```
in your script

```
unstuff <itemname>
[replace]
```

The "UnStuff" command UnStuffs or extracts the specified entries from the current archive and saves them to disk. It extracts all entries matching the <itemname>. Use this command when you want to UnStuff files or folders from an archive. You must have an open archive for the "UnStuff" command to work.

To UnStuff an entry from the current archive, use the line,

```
unstuff "Large File" replace
```
in your script

The files are saved in the last location set with the Destination command or to the same folder or level as the archive if no location has been set. You can save them to a different location using the Destination command. For instance, you could save them to the Graphics folder.

```
destination "Hard Disk:Graphics:"
unstuff "Large File" replace
```

---

unstuff «in» place <filename> [replace] [delete]

The "UnStuff in Place" command UnStuffs the entire contents of the specified archive. Use this command when you want to UnStuff an entire archive rather than individual entries. It is much more efficient than opening up the archive, UnStuffing all entries, and then closing the archive.

To UnStuff an entire archive and delete the original, use the line,

```
unstuff in place "Hard Disk:Archive.sit" delete
```
in your script

The files are saved into a new folder named, in this case, Archive Folder in the same folder or level as the archive.

---

use <filename>

The "Use" command allows you to direct commands to another open archive. It selects an open archive and makes it the "current archive." Use this command when you want to perform an operation on a different archive. This allows you to perform operations on several archives from one script.

All open archives should have unique names to avoid ambiguity when use the "Use" command.

To use another archive called The King.sit, enter the line

```
use "The King.sit"
```
in your script.

---

write status to <filename>

The "Write Status" command creates a file containing the diagnostic output for a script. If this command is not executed, a status file will not be created. Use this command when you are trying to diagnose script problems.

To create a status file, enter the line,

```
write status to "Hard Disk:Archive Diagnostics"
```
in your script.

If you do not specify a filename, StuffIt creates a status file with the same name as the script file and an ".out" extension. A new output file replaces any existing file with the same name.

Appendix: Common Questions (and Answers!)

General Questions

Q: Can you provide a simple explanation of how compression works?

A: Compression works by minimizing or eliminating redundancy and empty space. For example, the following 10 characters "AAAAAAABBB" could be stored in a file "as is" which would occupy 10 locations, or could be "encoded" as "7A3B" which would only occupy 4 locations resulting in a savings of 60%! StuffIt uses this very simple concept along with some complex compression algorithms to achieve excellent compression ratios at unbelievable speeds.

Q: What is an archive and why do I need one?

A: An archive is a file which acts as a container for files, folders, and disks. These items can be kept in an archive "as is" or they can be compressed and/or encrypted. StuffIt Deluxe is the application that creates and manipulates archives and their items. See "Chapter 1:Introduction" for a further explanation of an archive.

Q: How do StuffIt and SpaceSaver affect my System file or my System folder?

A: Neither StuffIt nor SpaceSaver ever modifies or affects your System file. This is one example of how StuffIt and SpaceSaver are extremely safe, perform completely reversible operations, and do not take control of your files from you. Some StuffIt and SpaceSaver files and folders are placed into your System folder so that other applications and utilities can find them easily. This is a standard Macintosh practice. StuffIt and SpaceSaver files can be found in the Extensions and Control Panels folders of your System folder, and within the Aladdin folder found in the Extensions folder. See "Where is StuffIt Deluxe Installed?," beginning on page 21, for further information.

Q: How do I send a compressed file to a friend who doesn't have any StuffIt product?

A: You'll need to send your friend a self-extracting archive which can be created in several ways. Using SpaceSaver, you can attach the ".sea" keyword to the file in the Finder. Using Magic Menu, you can select the file, and then choose "Make Self-Extracting". Using StuffIt Deluxe, you can check the "Self-Extracting" check box found in the lower left hand corner of the archive's window. You can also send your friend UnStuffIt.

Q: I installed the software and now my computer doesn't start up. What happened?

A: The software may be encountering problems with other Startup documents, Control Panel documents or System Extensions. On System 7, holding down the shift key when the Macintosh is starting will disable SpaceSaver and Magic Menu. Try removing your Startup documents, Control Panel documents, and System Extensions temporarily, and re-install them in your System Folder one at a time until you've found the incompatible file.

Q: May I give my co-workers a copy of this software?

A: No. This package is a commercial product and each copy can only run on a single computer. It is priced inexpensively enough so that anyone can afford a copy for their Macintosh. Aladdin Systems offers volume discounts and site licenses that are very reasonable for business users. Call us at (408) 761-6200 for details.

You may give UnStuffIt to your co-workers and friends so they can access SpaceSaver files and StuffIt archives you send to them. This is the only part of the package you can freely distribute as long as it is not for commercial use or profit. See "Chapter 9: UnStuffIt," beginning on page 171, for details on using UnStuffIt.

Q: I've read the User's Guide and I'm still having problems. What do I do?

A: Call our Technical Support Hotline at (408) 761-6200 between the hours of 9 am and 5 pm Pacific time. When calling our Technical Support Group, remember to:

• Know your hardware and software configuration (including the type of Macintosh, the amount of memory, and the startup documents, Control Panel documents, and system extensions installed).

• Know the version numbers of StuffIt, SpaceSaver, and the System Software you are using.

• Know the serial number of StuffIt.

• Have a detailed description of what happened.

• When possible, be seated at the Macintosh with the software running.

Q: I want to distribute my software product in a compressed, self-extracting form to save on diskette costs. Can I do this with my product?

A: Aladdin Systems licenses various types of self-extracting archives and installers. While a self-extracting archive is the simplest form of an installer, we have installation technologies that can automate a multiple disk installation process and more. Contact Aladdin Systems for more information.

StuffIt SpaceSaver Questions

Q: How do I know how much a file or folder was compressed by SpaceSaver?

A: Have the window open in which the file or folder resides. Choose "by Name" from the View menu in the Finder. The compressed size of the file or folder will be displayed in the Size column. Note that choosing "Get Info" from the Finder will sometimes expand the indicated item and therefore will not always show the item's compressed size.

Q: Can I create a "small" folder on a shared, network disk?

A: Yes, we call this feature a "SpaceSaver Server." However, anyone who wants to access compressed folders on server disks needs to have their own copy of SpaceSaver locally on their Macintosh.

Q: How do I prevent SpaceSaver from compressing individual files or folders that I don't ever want compressed?

A: Give those items a "big" keyword (or use a designated Finder label) and SpaceSaver will never compress those items.

Q: Will Idle Time Compression drain my Portable or PowerBook battery?

A: No. We have purposely disabled this feature when you are running under battery power. Idle Time Compression only works while the Macintosh is plugged in.

Q: I was using my computer and the power went out. When the power came back on, I started my Macintosh and immediately saw a message that said "SpaceSaver was unable to complete an operation. The temporary files are located in the Temporary Items folder within your Aladdin folder." What does this mean?

A: It means that SpaceSaver was compressing or decompressing when your power went out. Since SpaceSaver has multiple levels of protection against losing information, SpaceSaver placed some temporary files into a special folder. You will find this folder by following this 'path' to the file(s)—System Folder:Extensions:Aladdin:Temporary Items. Just move the file(s) that are there to another location, and then open them to see what the contents are. You'll find that you won't lose valuable information with SpaceSaver.

Q: When I open a folder containing many compressed Photoshop files, SpaceSaver appears to be working on them just to show the icons. What is happening?

A: Any software that embeds custom icons in documents will exhibit this. When the Finder needs to display the icon, SpaceSaver must expand the document to get the icon, and thus, the delay.

Q: Sometimes when I compress a file with SpaceSaver, it doesn't seem to get smaller. Why?

A: There could be a few reasons for this:

1) The file may be so small that, even after compression, it won't save any disk space so SpaceSaver simply doesn't touch the file;

2) The file may have the "big" keyword at the beginning or end of its name or the file resides within in a folder or disk with the "big" keyword;

3) The file may reside on a network disk and the "Never compress on remote disks" option is turned on;

4) The "Never compress on label" option is turned on and the file is labeled with the never compress label or one of its parent folders is labeled with the never compress label;

5) The file may reside on ejectable media (a diskette, for example) and the "Never compress on ejectable media" option is turned on;

6) You chose "Get Info" from the Finder's File menu. The Finder sometimes decompresses a file to access the required information to display. Use "View by Name" and look in the Size column for the compressed size.

7) SpaceSaver ignores certain types of files that are already compressed. Examples include QuickTime movies and files compressed using other compression products. Also, SpaceSaver will not re-compress a file that has already been compressed by SpaceSaver.

StuffIt Deluxe Questions

Q: Why are the buttons in the Archive Palette disabled when I first launch StuffIt Deluxe? I don't know what to do first.

A: The buttons in the Archive Palette represent common operations performed on the current archive. When StuffIt is first launched, there is no current archive. Begin by choosing "New Archive…" or "Open Archive…" from the File menu. See the tutorial "Example: Stuffing a File," beginning on page 45, in "Chapter 4: Using StuffIt Deluxe" for initial use of the Archive Palette.

Q: I stuffed multiple files into an archive and the archive is too large for a diskette. What do I do?

A: Segment the archive into diskette-sized pieces. See the tutorial "Example: Backing Up Your Yearly Archive," beginning on page 61, in "Chapter 4: Using StuffIt Deluxe" for more information.

Q: After Stuffing my files and folders into an archive, are the originals still on my disk?

A: Yes, unless you specifically instructed StuffIt to "Delete originals" or "Delete item when finished". For your protection, these options need to be specifically set by you. If you haven't set these options, the original items will still reside on your disk.

Q: Why do I have less space on my disk after using StuffIt to Stuff some files?

A: You still have the original files on your disk as well as the archive which contains compressed copies of those files. In order to save space on your disk, you need to delete the original files by putting them in the trash and emptying it.

Q: I received a StuffIt archive from a friend. What is a quick and easy way to access the files or folders contained with the archive?

A: There is more than one quick and easy way to UnStuff archives depending on which parts of the StuffIt package you have installed. Each of the following tools will UnStuff the items from an archive and place them into a single folder. If only one item exists in the archive, that item will be placed individually on your disk rather than being placed into a newly created folder.

• If you have Magic Menu installed, select the archive in the Finder and choose "Expand" from the Magic menu (or type Command-U).

• If you have Drop•UnStuff and are running System 7, drag the selected items in the Finder onto the Drop•UnStuff box. When Drop•UnStuff highlights, release the selection.

• In the StuffIt application, choose "Open Archive…" from the File menu, select the archive you want to UnStuff, and click "UnStuff".

• If you have SpaceSaver installed, remove the ".sit" extension from the end of the archive's name.

Q: What's the difference between StuffIt Deluxe and StuffIt Lite?

A: StuffIt Lite is a shareware product and is available from online services, user groups, and from Aladdin Systems. StuffIt Lite provides entry level compression, a small on-disk User's Guide, and covers basic concepts to give you a taste of the capability of StuffIt Deluxe. StuffIt Lite is a subset of StuffIt Deluxe, and does not incorporate many of the time saving and expert features found in StuffIt Deluxe. StuffIt Deluxe is a commercial product available from well known mail order vendors, from your local computer retailer, or directly from Aladdin Systems. StuffIt Deluxe has more convenient ways to create and manipulate archives than StuffIt Lite, includes a printed manual, Magic Menu, StuffIt SpaceSaver, and is the most complete compression solution available for your Macintosh.

Q: I've been using StuffIt 1.5.1, or StuffIt Classic. What's the difference between what I have and the latest versions?

A: StuffIt 1.5.1. is the shareware predecessor of StuffIt Classic, which is the shareware predecessor of StuffIt Lite. Those previous versions should be replaced with either the newer, faster, easier-to-use StuffIt Lite or StuffIt Deluxe. You should also refer to "StuffIt Converter," beginning on page 145, in "Chapter 7: The Tools/Utilities" for details on how to improve the compression of your older StuffIt archives.

Q: I downloaded a StuffIt archive from my favorite bulletin board system (BBS) and StuffIt won't recognize it. What's wrong?

A: Sometimes during the file transfer from a BBS to your Macintosh, a file gets modified in a way that makes StuffIt not able to recognize it. Before you download a file, make sure you have the "MacBinary" downloading option set in your communications application. If you have already downloaded an archive with MacBinary disabled, you can use the included MacBinary Translator to convert the file into a usable StuffIt archive. See "MacBinary," beginning on page 120, in "Chapter 6: Network/Communication Extensions" for details on decoding a MacBinary file.

Q: I dropped my hard disk and some of the files on it were damaged. How does my disk's bad media affect StuffIt archives, and how will StuffIt deal with these archives?

A: To the Macintosh, a StuffIt archive appears no differently than any other type of file such as a word processing file. While some applications don't allow you to open files which have been even partially damaged, StuffIt will make extra effort to open archives. StuffIt's built-in error checking may determine that an archive has been damaged and warn you accordingly. These archives will open as read-only, which means you may be able to UnStuff files but will not be able to modify the archive in any way. This method allows you as much access to your files as possible, giving you as much feedback as it can, without further endangering data in the archive.

Q: I received a Zip file from a friend who has an IBM-PC (or compatible). Can I do anything with it?

A: Yes. StuffIt Deluxe includes an UnZip Translator that can be accessed from the Translate menu. The UnZip Translator will give you access to the files contained in the Zip file. See "UnZip... (.zip), DeArc... (.arc), UnPack... (.pit)," beginning on page 112, in "Chapter 6: Network/ Communication Extensions" for information on UnZipping the file you have.

Q: I want to send a Zip file to a friend who has an IBM-PC (or compatible)? Can I do this?

A: No. The UnZip Translator that comes with StuffIt Deluxe can only decode Zip files. If you wish to send your friend a compressed file, send them a StuffIt archive and have them download UnStuff PC from an on-line service or BBS. UnStuff PC is Aladdin Systems freeware DOS utility for UnStuffing any StuffIt archive. If your friend doesn't have access to an on-line service or BBS, contact Aladdin Systems for information on obtaining UnStuff PC.

Q: If I choose "Open Archive..." to open a Compact Pro archive, StuffIt tells me the archive is damaged. What can I do?

A: You can expand the Compact Pro archive by choosing "CPT Extract..." from the Translate menu. See "CPT Extract...," beginning on page 111, in "Chapter 6: Network/Communication Extensions" for a tutorial on expanding the Compact Pro archive. You may also convert the Compact Pro archive into a StuffIt archive to save additional disk space by using the StuffIt Converter application. See "StuffIt Converter," beginning on page 145, in "Chapter 7: The Tools/Utilities" for use of that utility.

Q: I can't remember the password I used to encrypt some files in an archive. Can you help me?

A: No. StuffIt uses very secure encryption algorithms. It would be self-defeating to have a method to access the files without the password.

Q: What happened to the StuffIt Optimizers? Will I still have access to the optimized files in my current archives?

A: The ability to Stuff items into archives using file-specific optimizers has been removed from StuffIt to improve performance and efficiency. StuffIt will use the Optimizers you currently have in order to "de-optimize" and UnStuff an archive which contains optimized files.

Q: Why does my friend have a Script menu and I don't?

A: You don't have the Script menu enabled. Choose "Preferences" from the Edit menu to display the Preferences dialog. At the bottom of the dialog, you'll see some check boxes which enable and disable menus. Make sure that the Script menu check box is checked.

Q: When I click on the "Self-Extracting" check box, StuffIt tells me I can't turn the file into a self-extracting archive. Why not?

A: There are several reasons why you can't do this. One is that the archive is "read-only" which means that no modifications can be made to it. Try unlocking the file from the Finder's Get Info window, or unlock the disk it resides on, or move the archive to an unlocked disk. Another reason could be that the archive has items which were compressed or encrypted with a previous version of StuffIt. In this case, you'll need to UnStuff the contents from the older archive, create a new archive with the newer version of StuffIt, Stuff the items into the new archive, and then click the "Self-Extracting" check box.

Q: How can I make a segmented self-extracting archive?

A: Only archives can be made self-extracting. Segments cannot be made self-extracting. However, Aladdin Systems does provide similar functionality in our Installer Technologies for software developers and corporate users who wish to make the installation process easier for their users. Contact Aladdin Systems for details.

Q: I UnStuffed one file from an archive and then modified the file. How do I update the archive?

A: The archive still contains a copy of the original unmodified file. You should Stuff the modified file into the archive also. Then, at your discretion, you can delete the original file from the archive. Unlike the Finder, StuffIt archives allow multiple files with the same name in the same folder. This means you can keep a history of revisions in an archive.

Index

Numerics
1.5.1 archives 86
3.0 archives 86

Abort on error script command 178
Add Match
   Criteria 56
Add Match Dialog 54–58, 81–84
   Comments 82
   Date Created 84
   Date Modified 84
   Kind 82
   Label 83
   Name 82
   Size 84
Add Script 158
Aladdin Folder 22
algorithm (defined) 9
animated StuffIt cursor 34
Apple events 87, 165
AppleLink 28, 42, 138, 143
AppleLink Package Translator 109–111
AppleTalk Remote Access 40
.arc files 112
archive (defined) 10
Archive Menu 71, 91
Archive Palette 70–72, 87
Archive Window 72–77
   Comments Icon 74

   multiple 76
   pop-up menu 73
   Selecting Items 74
   Self-Extracting Check Box 74
   Status Area 74
   View Headings 74
ASCII to Binary Translator 118–120
Assign Command Keys (to script) 159
automatic compression
   defined 11
   using 28–32
automatic recompression 35

Balloon help 14
Basics of StuffIt 45
Batch Converting 145
big keyword 38
Binary to ASCII Translator 118–120
BinHex4 Translator 117–118
btoa/atob Translator 118–120

CE Software's QuicKeys 2 165
CE Software's QuickMail 124, 128
Change Password 64–67, 92
Claris XTND 147
Claris' HyperCard 168
clear match script command 178
close archive script command 178
Colorizing Palette Buttons 88
Comments dialog 78

Comments Icon 74
commercial distribution 189
Compact Pro 28, 42, 138, 143
Compact Pro Translator 111–112
compress
    on keyword 36–37
    on label 37–38
compressing
    files 25–26
    folders 23–25
compression
    choices 35
    defined 9
Compression Preferences
    (application) 93
Compression Primer 9
continue on error script command
    179
Convert 1.5.1 Archive 86, 92
Convert 1.5.1 Archives to 3.0 on Open
    86
Convert text file to Macintosh 122
Convert text file to PC 123
Convert text file to Unix 123
Converter 145–146
Converting AppleLink Packages 145
Converting Compact Pro archives 145
Converting Older StuffIt Archives 145
Copy/Move by dragging 59
Copying Button Colors 88
Copying graphics 105
Copying Viewer text 101
CPT Extract Translator 111–112
.CPT files 111
.cpt files 28, 42, 138, 143
Create 1.5.1 Archive 46
Custom Installation 19

Data integrity 34
data verification 34
DDExpand Translator 120
DeArc Translator 112–115
decode binhex script command 179
delete entry script command 179

delete file script command 179
Delete Item When Finished 56
DeluxeTop 60
destination script command 179
Detect Viruses With... 87
DiskDoubler files 120
diskette use 40
distribution of self-extracting files
    189
Don't Stuff Files That Are Already
    Compressed 85
dragging items 75
dragging onto buttons 71
Drop Boxes 135–137
    defined 12
Drop•Stuff 135–136
    defined 12
Drop•UnStuff 136–137
    defined 12

Easy Installation 15
Edit Script Menu 158
Editing a Script 155–157
ejectable media 40
encode binhex script command 180
Encryption 64–67
Encryption Preferences
    (application) 93
Erase Diskettes when Segmenting 62
Execute Script 157
executing commands 72
expanding multiple items 27–28
Extensions Defined 12

Fastest compression 35
file server use 40
Find text 101
Finder labels 37–38, 39
folders in title bar 73
forgotten passwords 64
FreeSoft's White Knight 129
Frontier 165

Generate Random passwords 65
Get Info window 80
good passwords 65

Help 14
Hide/Show Archive Palette 72
HyperCard XCMDs 168

Idle Time Compression
    defined 11
    using 28–32
Items to Stuff list 48

Join 61–63
join script command 180
Joining 63

Keywords 36–37, 38–39
    at beginning or end 24
    reserved 37
    rules 36

Label Menu 90
labels 37–38, 39
Last Window 77
Launch 53
launch script command 180
lost passwords 64

MacBinary Translator 120–121
Macintosh Programming Workshop
    169
Magic Menu 137–145
    AppleLink Packages 143
    Compact Pro Archives 143
    Compress 139
    defined 11
    Expand 138

Expand Preferences 142
Mail 125–126
Mail Preferences 127–128
Make Self-Extracting 140
Preferences 141–144
preferences 40–43, 141–144
Self-Extracting Preferences 144
Stuff 140
Stuff and Mail 126–127
Stuff Preferences 143
using to expand 27–28
Magic Menu and Electronic Mail
    124–128
make self-extracting preferences 43,
    144
manual
    compression 23–25
    expansion 27–28
match script command 181
Maximum Segment Size 62
Menus 89–93
MicroPhone II 129
MicroPhone II Scripts 129–131
Microsoft Mail 124, 128
monthly archives 54–58
Move/Copy 58–61
Moving the Archive Palette 72
MPW Tools 169
Multiple Archive Windows 76

Navigating an archive 73
network use 40
Network/Communication
    Extensions defined 12
never compress 31, 38–40
    on keyword 38–39
    on label 39
    on location 40
New Archive 45–49
new archive script command 181
New Folder 54–58
new folder script command 181
New Folder Suffix 87
Next Window 77

no status script command 181

On Location 147
On Technology's On Location 147
on/off 34
Open 49–52
open archive script command 182
Open dialog 69
Output Service 97

Package files 28, 42, 109, 138, 143
PackIt files 112
password length 65
Passwords 64–67
personalization 17
Personalizing StuffIt Deluxe 18
PICT Viewer 104–105
   Edit Menu 105
   File Menu 104
.pit files 112
.PKG files 28, 42, 109, 138, 143
PKZip files 112
Plus 168
Portable battery use 29, 189
postpone recompression 35
PowerBook battery use 29, 189
Preferences
   application 84–87
preferences 32–43
   Magic Menu 40–43, 141–144
   self-extracting 43, 144
   SpaceSaver Control Panel 33–40
Primer 9
Print Jobs 97
Printing PICT files 104
Printing Text files 100
progress
   dialog 34
   indicators 34

QuicKeys 2 165–168
QuickMail 124, 128
QuickTime movies 190
quit script command 182

Random passwords 65
read after write verify 34
Read Me files 49–52, 86, 97–100
recompress when idle 35
recompression 35
Record Script 93, 152–155
removable hard disk use 40
Remove Scripts 160
rename entry script command 182
rename file script command 182
Renaming items 59
reserved keywords 37
Retiling the Archive Palette 72

Sample Archive.sit 50
Save As Dialog 69
save as script command 182
Script Menu 93
Scripting 151–164
   Rules 175–178
   Variables 177
   Wildcards 177
.sea keyword 26
Securing Files 64–67
Segment 61–63
segment script command 183
Segment Sizes 62
Segment Suffix 62
Segmenting 61–63, 92
Selecting Items in Archive Window 74
Self-Extracting archives 67–68
self-extracting archives 26–27
   defined 10
Self-Extracting Check Box 74
server use 40
Service Bureau 97, 107

Show Archive Info In Window 94
Show Archive Palette 72
Show Sizes In K or bytes 94
Show Views 94
.sit keyword 27
small folders 25
small keyword 24, 25, 36
smallest compression 35
Software Ventures' MicroPhone II 129
SpaceSaver (defined) 10
SpaceSaver Server 189
spinning cursor 34
Stack Windows 77
startup icons 16
Status Area 74
status display 34
Stuff 45–49
stuff in place script command 183
Stuff Originals Instead of Aliases 85
stuff script command 183
Stuff XCMD 169
Stuffing a File 45
StuffIt Converter 145–146
    defined 12
StuffIt cursor 34
StuffIt Deluxe Folder 21, 46
StuffIt Deluxe Preferences file 85
StuffIt Menu Preferences (application) 89
StuffIt Primer 9
SuperCard 168
SyQuest cartridge use 40
System 6 and StuffIt 13, 15, 22, 29, 33, 37, 39, 80, 83, 85, 87, 90, 136, 145
System Folder 25
System Folder contents 22

Tab Width 103
tar Translator 115–117
Temporary Items folder 189
Text Convert Translator 122–124
Text Viewer 49–52, 100–104

Edit Menu 101
File menu 100
Find Menu 101
Font Menu 102
Size Menu 103
Tab Width 103
Tile Windows 77
title bar and folders 73
title bar pop-up menu 73
Tools/Utilities defined 12
transfer script command 184
Translate Menu 92
translate script command 184
Translating Different Data Formats 117–124
Translating Foreign Archive Formats 109–117
Translators 92, 107–124
Tutorial Files 47, 50

Unix tar 115
UnPack Translator 112–115
UnStuff 49–52
unstuff in place script command 185
unstuff script command 184
UnStuff XCMD 169
UnStuffIt 171–173
    defined 13
    using 171–173
UnZip Translator 112–115
use script command 185
UserLand Frontier 165
UUCode Translator 121–122

Verify 45–49
verify writes 34
View 'Read Me' Files on Open 86
View Headings 74
View Menu 90
View Preferences (application) 94
Viewer Extensions defined 12
Viewers 51, 97–105
Virus Checking 87

White Knight 129, 131–134
Window Menu 93
write status to script command 185

XCMDs 168
XTND 147
   defined 12

Yearly archive 58–61

Zip files 112